THE ART OF MONETARY POLICY

With a Foreword by William E. Simon

Richard V. Adams
Stephen H. Axilrod
Dewey Daane
Margaret Greene
Robert C. Holland
David M. Jones
Eugene A. Leonard
Bruce K. MacLaury

Scott E. Pardee
John Rau
Francis H. Schott
Robert Solomon
Peter D. Sternlight
Paul A. Volcker
Dennis Weatherstone
Albert M. Wojnilower

DAVID C. COLANDER
and
DEWEY DAANE
Editors

M.E. Sharpe
Armonk, New York
London, England

Library of Congress Cataloging-in-Publication Data

The art of monetary policy
edited by David C. Colander and Dewey Daane:
foreword by William E. Simon.
p.   cm.
Includes index.
ISBN 1-56324-346-6   ISBN 1-56324-347-4
1. Monetary policy—United States. 2. Monetary policy.
I. Colander, David C. II. Daane, J. Dewey (James Dewey), 1918–
HG501.A8   1994
332.4'773—dc20   93-45869
CIP

Printed in the United States of America

The paper used in this publication meets the minimum requirements of
American National Standard for Information Sciences—
Permanence of Paper for Printed Library Materials,
ANSI Z 39.48-1984.

BM (c) 10   9   8   7   6   5   4   3   2   1
BM (p) 10   9   8   7   6   5   4   3

THE ART OF MONETARY POLICY

To the memory of Alan Holmes, an outstanding example of the large cadre of public servants who have helped make this country great

Contents

Part III. Operational Details

Part IV. International Monetary Issues

Foreword

There are two important themes running through the essays in this volume. The first is the importance and excitement of public service. The second is that it is necessary to understand that monetary policy is an art, not an abstract science. This means that one must have an understanding of real-world monetary institutions in order to conduct meaningful debate about monetary policy. These are important themes with which Alan Holmes, the man to whose memory this book is dedicated, and in whose honor the essays were written, would have wholeheartedly agreed.

Alan Holmes and the Importance of Public Service

The price of wisdom, it has been written, is greater than gold, silver, and pearls. Alan Holmes was a man of few words, but infinite wisdom, whose knowledge and actions commanded respect and authority across the financial markets of the world.

Alan set a superior standard for public service during his thirty-one years of tenure and leadership in the Federal Reserve System focused at the Federal Reserve Bank of New York, the largest and most important bank in the Federal Reserve System. He directed the Federal Reserve Open Market operations and implemented the policies of the FOMC, the top monetary policymaking unit of the System. I will always remember and revere him as an outstanding central banker, a splendid colleague, and a warm, witty, and wonderful friend.

I was privileged to work with Alan while holding a number of positions that brought me into close contact with the Federal Reserve—as a senior partner at Salomon Brothers, a member of their Executive Committee in charge of government bonds, the U.S. Agency and Municipal Bonds Departments, as an adviser to the Treasury on debt management, and later as deputy secretary and secretary of the Treasury. Salomon Brothers and C.J. Devine were the two largest government bond dealers, and in that capacity were in constant contact with the Federal Reserve System and the Federal Reserve Bank of New York.

The Federal Reserve Bank of New York was the hub of Federal Reserve operational activity, both domestic and international, and as the person who manned its operations desk and carried out policies, Alan Holmes was literally at the nerve center of worldwide financial markets. He managed the day-to-day execution of the purchase and sale of U.S. government and agency securities in the open market, as well as swaps and foreign exchange. He had to have his finger on the pulse of all the markets. He traveled regularly to Basle, Switzerland, to meet with his counterparts among the leading central bankers of the world. The discussions were always shrouded in secrecy, of course, to guard the all-important confidentiality of their central bank interventions.

Alan was a key participant. He had a remarkable grasp of both the intricacies of monetary policy and the nuts and bolts of institutional and operational policy. He embodied the excitement of public service.

The Art of Monetary Policy

The way Alan approached monetary policy leads us to this book's second theme—the need to understand monetary institutions and to think of monetary policy as an art rather than a science. This second theme is not a new one, but it is one that is found in much of the early literature. For example, in his classic exposition, "The Art of Central Banking," R.G. Hawtrey clearly denotes that monetary policy is an art rather than a science. And so it is.

The essays in this volume make clear just how important it is to understand the art—the essence of the institutional and operational aspects—of monetary policy. I would emphasize that it is now more important than ever to recognize the nonmechanistic nature of monetary policy. Moreover, policy requires judgment at every stage of the process, from the initial formulation to the final implementation. And that judgment has to be exercised against the legacy of three decades of government profligacy that has saddled America with a $4 trillion public debt and chronic budget deficits, undermining the vitality of our economy and exacerbating difficulties of achieving stronger, noninflationary growth.

These frustrations, in turn, have intensified political pressures on the Federal Reserve—and most recently, on current Chairman Alan Greenspan—to continue easing interest rates further. Nevertheless, popular opinion to the contrary, inflationary considerations cannot be ignored. The intractability of long-term interest rates—which carry an inflation premium—are stark proof of the limitations of monetary policy to go beyond directly influencing the immediate level of short-term rates.

The lessons of our past, exacted at a steep price in lost incomes, production, purchasing power, and opportunity, are contained in the memories and experiences of our monetary artists. These lessons clearly prove that sound monetary policy is fundamental to a well-functioning economy, but they also prove that monetary policy is not the only game in town; indeed, without fiscal prudence, discipline, and restraint, the persistent easing of monetary policy will inevitably lead to higher, not lower, long-term interest rates and inflation. Today, even the hopes and expectations of overdue fiscal action have dramatically lowered long rates.

Monetary policy artists like Alan Holmes are increasingly confronted with political pressures in a world in which economics has too often become subservient to politics. One of the all-time great Federal Reserve chairmen, William McChesney Martin, always used to say that "good economics is good politics," and that if the Fed followed the right policy in the public interest the economic and political fallout would be favorable. But in today's world, good economics is seldom equated with good politics.

Probably the best way to illustrate the difficulty of pursuing the art of monetary policy in a political arena is to recount a couple of instances of past policy. Let us consider a case that directly affected me and in which Alan Holmes played a role. While much has been written about the so-called independence of the Fed as a necessary requisite of good monetary policy, the reality of political pressures is both real and intense. A classic case in Fed history occurred during the Johnson administration. In 1965, President Johnson embarked on a course of guns and butter, trying to fight two wars at the same time by simultaneously pursuing a sharp escalation of U.S. military spending on the Vietnam War and a burgeoning network of Great Society programs, accompanied by monetary expansion and then contraction.

Market watchers warned that LBJ's policies were sowing the seeds for an inflationary nightmare. And William McChesney Martin, Federal Reserve chairman at the time, was prompted to utter his famous remark, "I have to be the one who takes the punch bowl away at the party."

Apparently it was customary for chairmen to inform presidents of Federal Reserve policy actions before public release. The usual channels were either directly, or more commonly, through the secretary of the Treasury, and Chairman Martin had followed that practice. In December 1965, however, the Fed voted to tighten monetary policy and the chairman did not directly notify President Johnson, who was then out of town. When the president learned of the action (which was leaked in the *Washington Post*) he summoned Martin to his Texas ranch and flew into a rage, claiming "betrayal." Martin was a man of strength and firm principles and he would not be bullied. He stood fast.

What followed, months later however, was a classic credit crunch, and I remember experiencing its impact in a dramatic way from my own post at Salomon Brothers. We had positions in excess of $3 billion in various U.S. Treasury and agency securities. Obviously, positions of that magnitude rest on one's conviction that the market in Treasury securities will continue to be backed by ample liquidity to finance them.

I received a call from Robert Rivel, executive vice president of Chase Manhattan Bank, which was the prime banker in financing our security positions. Bob informed me that, henceforth, Chase Manhattan would limit its lending to Salomon Brothers to $25 million. To say I was incredulous would be the understatement of the century. I am very seldom at a loss for words, but I could barely question, "Why?"

Bob simply replied, "We're out of money."

Imagine what went through my mind at that moment. The Chase Manhattan Bank was out of money. Well, obviously, if you cannot finance your inventory, you not only cannot have inventory, but you also lose your ability to bid on government securities, Treasury bill auctions, and agency auctions and sales, and, again obviously, the markets would cease to function. The Treasury could not finance the new money it needed nor roll over and finance its existing debt—an unheard of, unthinkable dilemma.

The government bond dealers as well as thousands of institutional and individual investors were facing a full-blown financial crisis, with the potential for chaos in the markets that would have destroyed the government's credibility.

My first call was to Alan Holmes with the intention of explaining my conversation with Chase. I started out by saying, "Alan, I'll be sending all my boys over on Monday morning with wheelbarrows." To which he replied, "Bill, what are you talking about?" I then explained my call from Rivel. Alan did not hesitate a second or waste a minute. He immediately advised the Board of Governors of the Federal Reserve in Washington and acted to inject needed funds into the marketplace, simultaneously breaking the back of the credit crunch.

What a vivid impression that incident left with me. Alan Holmes knew what had to be done, and he did it. He was a true professional, and he confronted that crisis with the kind of expertise, boldness, and clear-eyed courage that Ernest Hemingway once described as "grace under pressure."

Today, nearly twenty-five years later, and much further down the road of fiscal excess, one must regretfully conclude that the more things have changed, the more they remain the same.

The Human Factor: Combining the Two Themes

The life and work of Alan Holmes combined this volume's two themes beautifully. As the Federal Reserve's eyes and ears, and right and left hands, Alan was an astute market man who conducted Federal Reserve policies with all of the confidence and aplomb of a concertmaster playing a Stradivarius violin.

Alan had intuition, judgment, absolute integrity, and above all, a humility that endeared him to everyone. For more than a decade, he carried out this nation's monetary decisions. He was an expert with few peers, who gained the acceptance, admiration, and praise of all those involved in the process—at the Treasury, the Federal Reserve, and in international markets across the world.

Central bankers are very often a misunderstood fraternity. They operate, by virtue of necessity, in a largely secretive world that many view as elitist, Byzantine, and bland. Alan Holmes was none of the above. He was, quite simply, one of the most skillful and experienced career civil servants I have ever known—a true professional, totally dedicated, and constantly mindful of the need to walk that fine line between divulging enough information to ensure smooth functioning in government securities markets and guarding the essential confidentiality of Federal Reserve deliberations and decisions which must never be breached.

Alan Holmes's task, as chief implementer of Federal Reserve policy, was to steer America's monetary ship through these difficult shoals. In doing this he was a true monetary artist. But he was more than an artist. He was a good person who cared about friendship and public service. I was indeed fortunate to have had the opportunity to work with Alan Holmes in so many incarnations. But most important, I was, and forever will be, honored by, and will cherish the memory of, my friend, Alan Holmes.

—William E. Simon
President, John M. Olin Foundation
Former Secretary of the Treasury

Acknowledgments

Bob Jones, a Middlebury College alumnus, endowed a chair at the college and named it the Alan Holmes Chair. Dewey Daane was the inaugural holder of the chair. As part of his inauguration, he arranged for a set of speakers to come to Middlebury and give students a picture of real-world monetary policy. The lectures were so stimulating and interesting that we decided to fit them into a book that would further honor Alan Holmes. This is the result, and we think it would make Alan Holmes proud.

Our thanks go first to Bob Jones; without him there would be no book. He has been a dedicated, energetic friend and benefactor of Middlebury College and its economics department. Second, we want to thank Jody Woos, who team-taught the inaugural course of which these lectures were a part. She shared with us a sense of the importance of real-world institutions; she made helpful suggestions on early drafts of the book, and would have been a coeditor but for other commitments. We are indebted to her for her contributions. Third, we want to thank our students, whose questions often sharpened the talks and focused the issues. Fourth, we would like to thank Tom Mayer and Raymond Lombra for their useful comments on initial drafts of portions of the book. Fifth, we want to thank Sheila Cassin, the economics department secretary at Middlebury. She handled most of the technical arrangements of the visits that made this book possible.

After the talks were presented came the task of making them fit together into a coherent whole. In this process, Helen Reiff played a significant role—transcribing, editing, restructuring, and offering advice about what works, and what does not.

At M.E. Sharpe, Dick Bartel guided the process, and Linda Frede-Tripicco was the production editor. Together with Helen Reiff, they turned the manuscript into a book.

While all the above people reduced our workload considerably, they did not eliminate it, and we want to give heartfelt thanks to our respective wives, Patrice Colander and Barbara Daane, for putting up with us as we lived in our academic heaven talking and arguing with the contributors, and to our children, who saw less of us than they otherwise would have.

Finally, and most of all, we want to thank the contributors, who gave selflessly of their time and effort to convey to our students and to the larger public their invaluable insights into the process.

THE ART OF
MONETARY
POLICY

Introduction: The Art of Monetary Policy

DAVID COLANDER AND DEWEY DAANE

Policy works because it has artists pulling the strings. This book is dedicated to one of those true artists, Alan Holmes. Holmes had a thirty-five-year career in public service, culminating in his position as the head of the Federal Reserve operations in both the domestic securities market and the foreign exchange markets. He was a genius at achieving policy consensus among disparate groups within the policy setting, making him both a formulator and an implementor of monetary policy. He understood both the highest level of theory and the most minute operational detail. The need for both policymakers and academic economists who write about policy to have this dual understanding is the central theme of this book.

It is a theme that is nicely illustrated by a story told by one of Holmes's colleagues, Paul Volcker. There was a squirrel in the forest who had a particular taste for fish. The squirrel went to the wise old owl for some guidance and counsel. After listening to his story, the owl advised the squirrel that the way for him to satisfy that desire was to become a kingfisher. So the squirrel happily went away, ran up a tree over a brook, and imagined himself a kingfisher so he could catch some fish. Of course, imagination was not enough. The squirrel discovered he was still a squirrel. After sitting in the tree for a while, he returned to the owl in a state of some agitation and railed, "You told me the way to satisfy my desire to get some fish was to become a kingfisher, but you haven't told me how to do that. I am still a squirrel." The owl replied, "Look, you came to me with a problem. I gave you some sound policy advice. The rest is operational detail."

We begin with this story because it captures the essential message of the book. *Understanding monetary policy requires an understanding of the operational details of monetary policy.* By operational details we mean more than just the technical means by which monetary policy is implemented; we mean the institutions and context within which policymakers approach an issue (for example, the existence of informal understandings and sensibilities that affect decisions) and the nuances of seemingly identical actions (the Fed buying Treasuries at 11:30 A.M. may mean something quite different than buying Treasuries at 1:00 P.M.).

It is necessary to know these operational details in order to do meaningful empirical work on monetary theory, to interpret data, and to choose between competing theories. If one does not know operational details yet is studying monetary theory or policy, one is playing irrelevant mind-games that may get one published, or through an exam, but that will have about as much meaning for the economy as the advice of the wise old owl had for the squirrel.

When Volcker told the story quoted above, he was picking on monetarists' single-minded focus on the money supply. The story, however, has broader relevance, and is directly applicable to many modern-day New Classical and New Keynesian monetary theorists, who, even more so than their predecessors, the monetarists and the various sorts of Keynesians, have lost sight of real-world institutions. Modern monetary theorists have become more and more deeply immersed in complicated theoretical constructs. The problem is that, complicated as these constructs are, they are nowhere near complicated enough; they lose many of the interactions and nuances that characterize the real-world institutions their theories purport to describe. This means that the subtleties of policy differences far exceed the subtleties of even the most complicated theories that can be taught to students. It follows that before such theories can be applied to the real world, these nuances and interactions must be included in the analysis. To do that in a meaningful way, one must have a deep sense of the institutions within which monetary policy is conducted.

Why do we belabor the obvious? Because much of the teaching of modern monetary theory and policy, both at graduate and undergraduate levels, has lost sight of the obvious. It is the teaching of theories and models—New Classical, New Keynesian, monetarist, global monetarist, neo-Keynesian, new-neo-Keynesian; there are many—without a meaningful operational context.

Instead of being taught that theories must be interpreted through a lens that reflects operational detail, students are taught to think through policy solely in relation to these models. They finish their courses with a knowledge of these models and the different strategies these models suggest for policy—you should use money supply as an intermediate target; you should use interest rates as an intermediate target; you should use a monetary rule; you should use discretion—and a belief that they can apply those models and the policies they studied to the real world.

That belief is an illusion. Few of the answers to specific questions about monetary policy depend on theoretical differences independent of institutional context. Most good policymakers could be monetarists one moment, Keynesians the next, and sometimes both simultaneously. They make decisions based on a sensibility and a feeling they have for the situation. That feeling and that sensibility are often related to their understanding of theories, but not in a straightforward way, at least not if they are good policymakers.

Let us give an example. One of the seminal ideas in New Classical economics was Finn Kydland and Edward Prescott's (1977) differentiation between a consistent and an optimal policy. An optimal policy is a policy that maximizes a social welfare function from a given point of time into the indefinite future. A consistent policy maximizes this same function, but is invariant over time. They showed that the consistent policy is preferable to the optimal policy.

The key insight that led them to their conclusion is that feedback effects of expected policy decisions can be important to current decisions; if future policy options are not restricted, individuals' current decisions will force policymakers to arrive at certain optimal, but, from a broader perspective, unreasonable, decisions. A good example is a child who wants ice cream and will scream incessantly if he or she does not get it. Let us say that the optimal policy is to give in. That might not be a reasonable policy. The consistent policy is to establish a rule from which it is impossible to deviate: No ice cream unless you eat your vegetables. Knowing that his or her parents cannot deviate from that rule, any rational child (and many real-world children) will modify his or her behavior, since the unmodified behavior will not produce ice cream and will make everyone worse off. The rule gets parents what they want and it involves less screaming, but this rule can only be implemented by limiting parents' discretion: they cannot give in, because they have made it impossible to do so.

This insight led Kydland and Prescott to a discussion of rules versus discretion in policymaking. In that discussion they equated rules with consistent policy, discretion with optimal policy, and proved that rules are preferred to discretion. They conclude:

> The implication of this analysis is that . . . active stabilization may well be dangerous and it is best that it not be attempted. Reliance on policies such as a constant growth in the money supply and constant tax rates constitutes a safer course of action . . . policy makers should follow rules rather than discretion. . . . One possible institutional arrangement is for Congress to legislate monetary and fiscal policy rules and these rules to become effective only after a 2-year delay. (Kydland and Prescott 1977, 476)

Kydland and Prescott's paper was seen as an important development in the academic debate about monetary policy. It was. New Classical economics, of which the Kydland and Prescott paper was one part, was a useful response to many neo-Keynesian models in which everything looked clear cut. Neo-Keynesians had used comparative static models to draw implications about what the appropriate monetary policy should be—interest rate control versus money supply targeting, for example. Kydland and Prescott's paper was useful in showing that any comparative static model will be insufficient to answer such questions, that the way in which individuals form expectations, and how those expectations interrelate with policy, makes a difference in answering such questions. Like the game of scissors/rock/paper, these New Classical models covered neo-Keynesian models, which themselves had covered earlier monetarist black box models.

But all of these academic mind-games are quite irrelevant to the debates about the conduct of monetary policy. Kydland and Prescott's proof of the superiority of rules over discretion is based on an assumption that one can have fully specified contingent rules. Unfortunately, because the future is unknown, the assumption cannot be met in the real world. Even coming close to meeting it—designing a contingency rule for all currently conceivable contingencies—is too costly to implement. Any real-world rule must be of limited contingency. For some contingencies you will want a rule; for others you will not. There is no general proof about the superiority of limited rules versus discretion.

There is no escaping the need for situation-dependent judgment.

If one looks at the conduct of real-world monetary policy, it is clear that monetary policy has always been conducted with a distinction between optimal and consistent policy and with a deep understanding of dynamic feedback effects, just as most parenting is conducted with that same deep understanding. All policymakers, even parents with ice-cream-hungry kids, attempt to have rules. But every policymaker, and every economic agent, recognizes that rules can be broken depending on the situation.

The art of parenting is to impose your rules in a way that does not lead your child to total rebellion, while at the same time instilling in your child those values you want to instill (and to do it with children who also know the value of the "Cry until you get ice cream" rule, which seems to be instinctually conveyed at birth). The art of monetary policy is in finding the appropriate rule of limited contingency and in distinguishing those situations in which a rule can usefully be broken— because the situation is a sufficiently unique historical event, or one with such long-run consequences that there will be no long run unless the rules are broken—from those situations that can be dealt with by rules. For example: Should the Fed bail out large banks? If it does, or can be expected to do so, the large bank will build that into its expectations, making it more necessary to bail out such banks. If the Fed does not bail out the large bank, the entire financial system may collapse. Alternatively, should a parent relent and give ice cream to a child who is dying from cancer? These are extreme examples, but deciding which case is typical and which case is not is a judgment call; no theory can lead to an answer.

The Scribblings of Real-World Practitioners

We put together this volume because of the current separation between theory and real-world policy. The essays in it are not the scribblings of academics; they are the scribblings of real-world practitioners—the artists of monetary policy. By bringing together essays by some of the most talented artists in the field, we hope to begin to build bridges between theory and practice; we hope to help students, who will become the future theorists and policymakers, get a better sense of the institutions and operations that are so fundamental for an understanding of monetary policy. We hope to give them an entrée into the art of monetary policy.

Using one's knowledge of theory combined with one's knowledge of the relationships and institutions to make reasonable decisions about monetary policy is what we mean by the art of monetary policy. You cannot get that operational knowledge from studying models or theory, no matter what the flavor; you get it from studying institutions and their development. You get it from apprenticing yourself to those public servants who know the institutions, and to those people who have thought about them and immersed themselves in understanding them. Clearly, this is not the content of most economics students' training, whether it be at the graduate or the undergraduate level. And that is a major flaw in economics students' training.

To tie one's hands in the hope of taking advantage of rules over discretion is also to tie one's hands in cases where discretion is called for. Kydland and Prescott's "seminal" work lagged far behind real-world decision making; with it, academic economists' modeling techniques simply narrowed the lag between academic theoreticians and practitioners.

The Consequences of Teaching Theory Without Art

The current practice of teaching students theory without art hurts both theory and policy. Theory is hurt in one way—it becomes theory for the sake of theory, theory unconnected to reality; policy is hurt in two ways—many potentially superb policymakers do not go into policy, and the policy that is conducted does not have the benefit of informed theory. Let us first consider how theory is hurt.

How Theory Is Hurt by Current Practices

Many graduate students in monetary economics go on to distinguished academic careers proving lemmas and theorizing about issues such as whether rules are better than discretion, whether monetary aggregates are preferable to interest rates as intermediate targets, how to add an equation to a model to make it come up with a different answer, or how to test empirically whether this model or that model is preferable. This work is far less meaningful than it could be because many of these theorizers have no training in the art of applying economic models to policy issues. They try to squeeze answers out of theory that cannot be squeezed out. Theory without a deep sense of the institutions does not answer policy questions.

We are not arguing against theory or theorizing. Once people have information about the way the system actually works, they can generalize from it; they can simplify and condense their insights, and come up with relevant and useful models that embody their insights and knowledge. But those models do not have an existence independent from their creator's knowledge of the way the real world works. To judge whether a model is useful requires insights and institutional knowledge. A model is simply a key that opens the door to the much more complicated and messy real world. It is not a world unto itself. Keynes summarized the issue nicely when he said, "Economics is a science of thinking in terms of models joined to the art of choosing models which are relevant to the real world."

Because of the nature of the model as a simplified representation of reality, it generally cannot be formally empirically tested in a meaningful way; the model is part and parcel of a larger vision. A model has meaning only with the large number of ad hoc assumptions and provisos in the back of the modeler's head that reflect that vision. If an empirical observation does not fit the model, the model will be adjusted to the vision. Understanding the vision behind the model is as important as understanding the model.

The Monetarist Vison and the Keynesian Vision

Consider the monetarist and Keynesian visions. The monetarist vision is of a political climate in which government will too often give in to political pressures, will take the easy way out, and will consistently err on the side of using too much discretion. The Keynesian vision is of a political climate in which government will operate reasonably effectively even in the face of political pressures; while it might sometimes take the easy way out, it will generally conduct policy for the common good. The differences in monetarist and Keynesian policy proposals follow from the differences of those visions, not from any economic model. Yet the monetarist and Keynesian visions have seldom been discussed, and academics have forced the differences to show up in the shape of some curve or specification of a model.

What has happened is that Keynesian and monetarist models, freed from the institutional knowledge of their creators, acquired a life of their own. An equation was added here, a term reinterpreted there, and pretty soon, one had a model with little or no relation to the vision. Moreover, as institutions changed, so too did the appropriate models to describe them. It would seem reasonable that sometimes the Keynesian vision fit reality and sometimes the monetarist vision fit reality. Given the changing problems and institutional structure, the two visions are not necessarily incompatible.

How many economics students are currently taught to view theories in this way? Few, we believe. Instead they are taught that one or the other theory must be right, and that the choice between the two must be made on the basis of formal empirical tests. When, instead of informal empirical tests of the larger vision, formal empirical tests are used to determine which model is preferable, the winning model becomes merely the result of a competition, with the winner determined by the ingenuity and perseverance of researchers in various groups. If you lose one round, you simply modify an ad-hoc assumption and win the next until the debate fades away.

Has forty years of empirical testing determined whether the monetarist or the Keynesian model is the correct one? Does anyone believe that a definitive test exists? Instead of conclusively answering such questions, theorists simply pose new ones; thus the academic debate has shifted from a monetarist/Keynesian debate to a New Classical/New Keynesian debate. (The latest fad is to look for unit roots, in an attempt to test whether a data series generating function is, or is not, stationary. Unfortunately, as every artist knows, the future may be different from the past, so even if an answer is forthcoming based on past data, it will not definitively answer the policy question.)

Art and the Comparative Advantage of Educational Institutions

Many academics agree with us about the above arguments, but nonetheless argue that educational institutions should focus on models. They argue that universities have a comparative advantage in teaching science rather than art, theory rather than mundane operational details and insightful knowledge. How the world really works, they claim, is learned as much by osmosis as by teaching. They argue, "You don't teach artists by teaching them art theory; you teach them by having them practice, correcting them when they are wrong, showing them how to do it; and, then, once they've learned how to do what can be done, you show them how to experiment and go beyond the current state of the art. The only way one learns the institutional sense necessary to judge models is to work in the institutions—to get a feel for those institutions and a sensibility about them—the university is not the place to get that."

We agree with the sensibility of such critics, but disagree with the conclusion. We believe that undergraduate and graduate schools can teach art, and that doing so would significantly improve economic education. True, art is best learned in real-world institutions, but that does not preclude it from being taught in the classroom.

Even if it is extraordinarily difficult to teach art, the conclusion—that because of academic economists' comparative advantage, they should teach only theory—does not follow. Such a conclusion would follow only if all graduate education in economics required a real-world apprenticeship in which all theorists gained first-hand knowledge of the real world. But that does not happen; no undergraduate or graduate economics program that we know of has such an apprenticeship program. Unless the art of economics is taught in graduate school, even taught badly, it will not be taught.

Unfortunately, the current situation is not only that the art of economics is not being taught. It is worse; graduate schools are not even teaching that it is important. Currently, students are given no sense of the limitations of what they are doing.

Thus, we believe that at a minimum, *it is still fundamentally important to teach students that the art of monetary policy is important, and that it is a necessary component of understanding the models, of testing models, and of working with the models.* The danger of not teaching the importance of the art of economics is that the students start seeing the model as the reality and they lose any interest in the reality that model is supposed to describe.

How Policy Is Hurt by Current Practices

As we stated above, policy is hurt in two ways by current practices. The first way it is hurt has to do with the number of people planning to go on to work in policy. Many economists trained by academic institutions do, of course, go into policy jobs. The initial transition is difficult, but successful transfers quickly learn to forget most of what they learned in graduate school. It was a hurdle they had to get over to get to policy; not a necessary part of their training. And since one has to be bright to get over that hurdle, graduate schools serve as a screen for job applicants. In a good policy environment it takes about two months for a bright economist to learn that much of his or her graduate training is irrelevant to the real issues, and another two years or so to get a sense of the institutions and insights of current policymakers. So the system works, but it does not work as well as it could.

One reason the system does not work as well as it could is that many people who would make wonderful policymakers never go into policy at all. Schools operate like a filter and they are screening out large numbers of people. What happens is that potentially brilliant artists never become policymakers. Alan Holmes was a true artist; he had the integrity, the judgment, and a well-honed sense of how theory can be interpreted to be relevant to the real world. People like him make a system work. One of the most important jobs an educational system can fulfill is to train and prepare people like Holmes to go into public service. Our educational system is not fulfilling that role.

Let us give an example. When Paul Volcker gave a speech at Yale, he asked some 350 or so students how many planned to go on into public service. The result: only one student said that he had such plans, and Volcker was not sure that student understood the question. Graduate schools in economics are no different. In interviews Klamer and Colander (1990) conducted with graduate students at top schools, many graduate students said they were talked out of going into policy work, even though the reason they had gone to graduate school in the first place was to prepare themselves for policy work. "Policy is for simpletons" is the view they heard from their teachers.

This does not mean that academics actually come out and say that policy is for simpletons (although some of the less discreet of them do say it), but it is the view that the students hear and absorb. By the end of three years of graduate economic education, most students are socialized into the academic way of thinking and are directed away from any policy work.

Again, Paul Volcker has a story that captures the problem. After leaving the Fed, he taught at Princeton. While there he was swamped with work and asked a junior colleague to assist him with a book he had agreed to do. The young colleague said no, that he could not work on a book on policy because it would ruin his career. Paul was surprised and later asked the departmental chairman if that were true. The departmental chairman thought for a moment and said, no, not if the young colleague did it only once.

The second way that policy is hurt by the current situation is that policy is robbed of the useful insights that would come from relevant and informed theorizing and modeling. Keynes once said that we are all slaves of some defunct economist, and by that he meant some defunct economic theorist. Policymaking is based on an implicit or explicit vision of how the economy works. Ultimately, theory lies behind that vision; theoretical advances help sharpen policymakers' vision. When theory is doing its job, theorists' work acts as a corrective lens on policymakers' visions, placing issues in different focus. Different theories provide a different focus on issues. Ultimately, policymaking requires an integration of the different visions that flow from different theories.

When theorists no longer relate their theories to visions, policymaking suffers. Currently, the vision taught to policymakers in their on-the-job training is the existing institutional vision. The students who come to work in policy are essentially *tabulae rasae*. They often have learned little in graduate school that cannot be quickly shown to be foolish or irrelevant. Because they have not developed their own judgment, after their on-the-job training is complete they are generally imprinted with the establishment vision. In the United States this means that a particular Fed vision is the one currently informally imprinted on incoming policymakers. The Fed vision may be right. But unless people trained in the art of policy outside the Fed interrelate with that vision, the Fed vision will tend to perpetuate itself, whether it be right or wrong. Currently, except within the Fed itself, there is little meaningful interaction of alternative visions that can lead to major policy changes and innovations.

The Essays in This Volume

This volume is meant as a small step in reintroducing the art of monetary policy and its relationship to the economy to students and theorists. It is a collection of essays by practitioners of monetary policy conveying their vision of how monetary policy and the economy work. All the essays were written in honor of Alan Holmes, who epitomized the professional policymaker. They were delivered to a senior economics seminar at Middlebury College, and the contributors were asked to maintain an informal presentation style so that their thoughts would be accessible to a wide range of readers.

Part I

Part I considers the problem of monetary policy in its broadest dimensions. The first essay, "The Human Factor and the Fed" by Paul Volcker, nicely captures the importance of the art of monetary policy. In it, Volcker points out the simple, but often forgotten, truth that central banks are human institutions; monetary policy is made by people, not machines or computers. Because the central bank is often called upon to do unpleasant things, the integrity of the people working in central banking is of central importance. They have to be able to make hard decisions in the face of difficult political pressure.

The second essay, "Change and the Art of Monetary Policy" by Dennis Weatherstone, gives you a sense of how policy is undertaken and the importance of institutional structure. Weatherstone points out how one cannot understand monetary policy or test what theory is correct without understanding the institutional structure within which it is conducted. He explains how, until recently, the Bank of England operated with few rules, but a strong "eyebrow policy," while the U.S. Fed used a more formal approach to rules. Both regulatory environments worked, but they worked quite differently. He then talks about the problem of coping with change—how technological changes continually undercut existing regulations and require continuing changes in the regulatory environment. His discussion brings home the point by considering derivatives and the problems of finding an appropriate way to regulate these new financial instruments.

The third essay, "The Limitations of Monetary Policy" by Robert Holland, discusses the limitations of monetary policy. Holland argues persuasively that societies often call upon central banks to do more with monetary policy than can be done, and that a careful and realistic analysis of the structural limitations of monetary policy is a necessary foundation to understanding monetary policy. He goes on to list three general categories of limitations: human capability limitations, institutional structural limitations, and economic structural limitations. If we forget these limitations, and ask too much of monetary policy, not only will monetary policy not succeed in achieving any additional goals we assign it, it will also not achieve the goals it can achieve.

The fourth essay in Part I is "A Primer on the U.S. Banking Situation" by Albert Wojnilower, who argues that in the United States we have failed to regulate our financial institutions properly and by such failure we have "destroyed the ability of our banking system to support and foster the development of risky enterprises." This failure will slow economic development, and future generations will pay the price. Wojnilower concludes with the suggestion that we "think of our banking problem as not essentially financial, but rather as a particular manifestation of an awesome challenge that all the world now faces: how to organize, in a modern sociopolitical setting, economic systems that can mobilize the strengths of both competition and cooperation, despite the propensity of each to destroy the other."

The final essay in Part I is by John Rau. He argues that by the year 2000 there will be enormous structural and technical changes in banking both domestically and globally and that if regulatory reform in the United States does not keep pace with these changes, "we will end up with a system that cannot compete internationally. . . . Either we keep up, or we lose out. There are no other choices." He reviews the history of bank consolidation over the past decade and discusses the various phases of this consolidation. He argues convincingly that banks will have to develop their special niche, unbundling services, expanding those they perform well, and eliminating those they do not.

Combined, these essays provide an excellent overview of the current challenges facing monetary policy and the problems we will likely have in meeting them.

Part II

Part II, entitled "Real-World Policy," consists of three essays. In the first, entitled "The Fed: Reconciling Autonomy and Democracy," Bruce MacLaury discusses the political problems central banks face. He lists four reasons why central banks are controversial and unpopular, and gives his views as to why that will not change. He distinguishes between big and little politics and explains how the current institutional structure of the Fed reflects both. He then goes on to show how policy can best be understood within this political context.

In the second essay, "Monetary Policy as Viewed by a Money Market Participant," David Jones gives some fascinating insights into the art of monetary policy as seen through the eyes of a Fed watcher who is involved in interpreting Fed policy every day. Jones explains the real-world conditions that lead any forecaster away from the science of economics and into the art of economics. He argues that in order to understand the effect of policy on the economy, one must understand not only the data and the effect of changes in data on the economy, but also the way in which the policymakers react to data changes. He shows how a complete knowledge of the Federal Reserve institutional structure and operational detail is absolutely necessary for understanding monetary policy and the economy.

The final essay, "A Monetarist's Confession" by Eugene Leonard, explains what monetarism is, and why Leonard believes it is the best way to understand the economy. He accepts the argument that monetarism is a "black box" theory, but argues that because of the complex institutional structure of the real-world economy any theory must necessarily be a black box theory. Since abstract theory can guide us only so far, we must rely on a knowledge of monetary history to guide our policy decisions. Given a knowledge of monetary history, Leonard argues that the monetarist position, interpreted with modern institutional knowledge, is on solid ground.

Part III

Part III concerns the operational details of monetary policy. The first essay, "The Implementation of Monetary Policy" by Peter Sternlight, provides a glimpse of the operational detail that is necessary for a meaningful understanding of monetary policy. In it, Sternlight details his career path to the head of the open market desk at the Fed. He explains how particular operating techniques have evolved over time and how practitioners have moved to a middle ground between rules and discretion. He describes the operating policy of affecting nonborrowed reserves, and how that policy works within the institutional structure. He shows how what might "seem like a fairly mechanistic sort of operation is not that at all" and how "even the most routine daily decision requires an element of judgment."

The second essay in Part III, "Debt Management" by Richard Adams, provides the operational detail about the market in which open market operations work—the government debt market. Adams reviews who the major investors in the market are and how the market works, and discusses some of the rules relevant to the market. He concludes with a discussion of some issues relevant for reform of the auction process by which the Treasury sells bonds.

The third essay in Part III, "The Federal Open Market Committee in Action" by Dewey Daane, provides a ringside seat at an open market committee meeting where monetary policy decisions are made. Daane discusses the structure of the meeting, the interaction of the members of the committee, and the three Fed policy books that contain the staff input into the decision.

Part IV

As was emphasized by many of the essays in the previous sections, the big story for monetary policy in the 1990s will almost certainly be centered on international issues. Part IV considers these. The first essay, "The Globalization of World Financial Markets" by Stephen Axilrod, argues that in the 1990s the financial world will become increasingly globalized by four phenomena: deregulation, changing laws, the continuing growth of Japan in the global financial market, and the emergence of new financial technology. In this globalized market, "some major markets may for a while remain out of line with others, but they will eventually be brought into line," and the need for international economic cooperation will be stronger than ever.

The second essay, "A Trader's View of the Foreign Exchange Market" by Scott Pardee, provides an inside description of the foreign exchange market by one of the traders in that market. Pardee describes some of the strategies that traders use and gives the reader a real feel for the market which no one except an insider could give. Pardee concludes with a wonderful story that both instills a sense of being a trader and explains why "it's a little different in the real world than it is in theory, and anyone who is trying to understand international monetary issues must understand both the real world and theory."

The third essay, "Monetary and Exchange Rate Policy Implementation" by Margaret Greene, provides a different perspective of the foreign exchange market. Greene explains the linkage between domestic monetary policy and the exchange rate in both theory and practice, a practice much more complicated than theory can take into account.

The fourth essay, "Fixed versus Fluctuating Exchange Rates" by Francis Schott, nicely describes a hardy perennial topic in economics. In it, Schott explains why this is a perennial topic and why it will remain one. He discusses the trend toward economic integration and concludes that even as the discussion of the terms and conditions of economic integration are showing signs of progress toward a unified and interdependent world economy, the argument over fixed versus fluctuating rates is becoming a less heated one.

The final essay of the book, "International Coordination of National Economic Policies" by Robert Solomon, reiterates the belief that the central economic issue of the 1990s will concern the global interdependence of economies. In his essay, Solomon discusses the need for international policy coordination and then gives some examples of the lack of coordination in the past. He then discusses some imagined obstacles to integration and explains why these are not really obstacles, but tells us how other, real, obstacles do exist.

Conclusion

None of the essays in this volume is highly technical. Economics students at various levels should be able to follow all of the theory in them. But the insight they provide into policy and the problems of monetary policy is deep. They give one a better sense of the depth of real-world monetary policy than do most graduate courses in monetary theory and policy. They are written by the true artists of monetary policy, and we believe Alan Holmes would have been pleased by their message.

References

Klomer, Arjo, and David Colander. *The Making of An Economist.* Boulder: Westview Press, 1990.

Kydland, Finn, and Edward Prescott. 1977. "Rules Rather than Discretion: The Inconsistency of Optimal Plans." *Journal of Political Economy* (June):473–91.

Part I

General Issues

1

PAUL A. VOLCKER

The Human Factor and the Fed

Structurally, the Federal Reserve is a very peculiar organization. Designed for public purposes, it retains some private participation; while policy needs to be uniform around the country, the formulation has important regional elements. There is nothing else in government quite like it. It has a chairman, but he is only one member of a seven-person Board of Governors in Washington. The System also has twelve Federal Reserve Banks with an unusual appointment process for presidents, which many people never understand even when you explain it to them.

All these officials have some legal responsibility for policy; aided and abetted by highly professional staffs, they all have some desire to influence policy. And they do, but in a very complicated process that you must be a part of to truly understand. In the end, however, the various views must be assimilated and reduced to directives to some person who has to implement a single policy in a way that affects the whole country. The policy is carried out in quite measurable, concrete ways, typically by buying or selling securities, or buying or selling foreign exchange in the market.

The decision to buy or sell so many securities on a particular day at a particular time in response to the policy directive is the responsibility of the manager of the Federal Open Market discount window. That decision may sound straightforward and rather mechanical. Making and implementing those decisions, however, requires enormous skill. Not only must one fully understand the mechanics and nuances of the market, one must be able to maintain relationships of mutual confidence with the people who view themselves as policymakers. I assure you that (at least from my unique and totally unbiased point of view) it was very easy when I was chairman of the Board! But when Arthur Burns was chairman, and one of the editors of this volume, Dewey

Daane, was on the Board of Governors, and other strong-minded people with conflicting views were looking over each others' shoulders, it took a real genius in human relations! Alan Holmes, the person this book honors, was that genius.

Alan Holmes—The Ideal Public Servant

Alan Holmes was a wonderful man. He epitomized the professional civil servant. All his life—literally all his working life—he spent in the Federal Reserve Bank of New York, moving up the ladder from one position to another. He started out as an international economist and ended up managing both foreign exchange and domestic securities operations for the Federal Reserve, the key operating position and, in effect, the direct transmission belt from policy to the market. In that role, he not only had great technical skill and understanding, he also had a gift for human relations.

No one can last in such a job without being able to get along with people. Alan had to reconcile contrasting and compromised policy views into coherent operations. Policy can be effective only when the people who carry out that policy are faithful to its purposes and can also work with their colleagues and those immediately affected by the policy—in Alan's case, these people were money market and foreign exchange managers and professionals within the Fed, the Treasury, and private institutions.

Alan Holmes had great personal integrity and honesty. Now obviously, these are qualities any human being would like to have. But they are particularly important for a central banker and public servant conducting operations where discretion and confidence are essential to the successful execution of policy.

The Human Factor in Government

I discuss Alan Holmes's traits because they shed light on how a central bank really works. Central banks are human institutions. Like other human institutions, how they are led and how they are staffed makes a difference for policy in both a technical sense and in the larger sense of its overall coherence.

When I left the government, I briefly headed up the Commission on the Public Service. This Commission was made up of a group of distinguished people from all over the political spectrum, including ex-presidents, ex-senators, chief executive officers, college presidents, and particularly men and women with experience in the executive branch of the federal government. The members shared one thing in common: a concern that the basic competence—the skill, the expertise, and to some degree the integrity—of civil servants was declining. The result was contributing to the growing lack of trust and credibility in government itself. This, the Commission felt, was not good enough for the country. We addressed the question: what could be done about it?

The Commission members tended to be in their late fifties or in their sixties, with one or two older. This meant we came from a time when the attitudes toward government were quite different from what they are now. We remembered World War II and the immediate post-war period when the United States saw itself undisputed leader of a shattered world, with confidence that it had sound ideas as to how that world should be run. We thought we as a nation had ideas about how to avoid repeating the depression that was characteristic of the 1930s, and how, internationally, to encourage peace and greater harmony at least among the nations of the "Free World." It was a time of great creativity in which many of the international institutions we take for granted were created: the IMF, the World Bank, the GATT, the United Nations itself—all in one great burst over the course of two or three years. Only a little later there was the great initiative of the Marshall Plan. It was a period of growing faith in economics, and economists came to think that maybe they could develop the way to avoid serious recessions, to deal with inflation, to eliminate poverty, to protect against the vicissitudes of old age, and all the rest.

The time period we on the Commission remembered was one in which young people were intrigued with the idea of going into government and making a difference. Government service was the career choice of many bright and energetic young people.

Unfortunately, that is not true today—certainly not to anything like the same extent. People still want to make a difference, but today they think, or at least they have until recently, that the way to make a difference is to go make some money in Wall Street or become a lawyer or maybe become a scientist. Government service is not high on their list. In fact, it is not quite respectable to be in government. I may be exaggerating a bit, but a survey of Yale seniors a few years ago suggests that this is not much of an exaggeration. In this survey, 357 students were asked if they had any interest in going into government. One out of the 357 said that he might have some interest. (I always thought he probably did not read the question correctly.)

Things may be a little better now, but not much, which means that the country has a serious problem. I will not discuss all the ins and outs of this problem in this essay.[1] But I submit to you that an effective government and an effective country depend on there being some credible institutions that can be trusted. This requires that they have competent people of integrity willing to work for them over a substantial period of time. That is simple common sense. While the central bank is not so widely known, I think it is important that it be one of those credible institutions.

Professionalism in Central Banking

Central banks must command trust, they must be credible, and they must have integrity because they are often called upon to do unpopular things. Central banks can and do create money, and the power to create money implies great temptations for governments. Too much money means inflation, and those who manage central banks must exercise restraint on the money supply in the face of political pressures. There is some universal instinct that says to people around the world, "Don't let politicians run the printing press." There is a lot of history and reasoning behind that almost instinctive judgment. Politicians are always tempted to spend money on things that please their constituents. Left unbridled, politicians find it is hard to resist the pressures because there is, indeed, always a lot to be done. The problem comes in the paying. So there is an insidious temptation to try to resolve all the dilemmas and priorities by creating more money to finance the programs they have in mind—creating it either directly or by creating budget deficits.

That is where central banks come in. If they have a degree of independence, they can control the printing press. Elected representatives and the executive are one step removed from direct control over monetary policy.

That desire to achieve some separation of the printing press from day-to-day political pressure accounts in large part for the peculiar structure of the Federal Reserve. But this desire for some insulation from direct political pressure is manifest in varying degrees in other countries as well.

If a degree of insulation or independence from partisan or narrow political pressure is to be maintained, there needs to be a high degree of trust and confidence by the people that the responsibility for monetary policy will be shouldered without fear or favor. No law will achieve independence if that essential degree of trust and confidence is lost. The legal structure simply will not last politically—nor, in those circumstances, should it. So it is particularly important that a central bank attract and nurture people like Alan Holmes—true professionals who know what they are doing, but who, at the same time, are dedicated to the public interest and faithfully carrying out the decisions of the policymakers.

Two Examples of the Importance of Structure

I have referred to the importance of insulation from "passing" political pressures. No central bank can—or should, in my judgment—conduct policies for long that are out of keeping with basic, continuing objectives of the political system, broadly construed: objectives such as the desire to moderate the business cycle, to fix exchange rates, to combat inflation, and the like. But within a central bank's broad mandate, independence can be maintained, and that is greatly assisted by the fact that central banks generally are self-financing. The reality is that printing money is a very profitable activity; if you have a monopoly on money creation and you can keep some of the profits—the seigniorage—then you have budgetary discretion. When an institution has that privilege, it must be controlled and disciplined by an inner professionalism, and that inner professionalism may be far more important to the success of a central bank over time than any of the technicalities of monetary policy. Let me give you two examples, the Bank of Mexico and the Bank of Italy.

Forty or fifty years ago Mexico was a poor, underdeveloped country. It did not have a tradition of strong economic institutions, professionalism in government, or even great competence, for a variety of reasons not unique to Mexico. But the Mexican central bank, which historically had a tradition of being a little apart from the rest of the government, undertook to nurture professionalism and independence within itself. It did so even while its monetary policy could be directed by the government.

One governor in particular, a man by the name of Gómez, made a practice of hiring the best young people he could find out of Mexican universities—four, five, six a year. He would finance their education abroad—in those days that was usually here in the United States, but they could go elsewhere. He would guarantee them a job; in fact, he would provide them with a career "home" if they went off and did another important job within the government, as many of them did. Within twenty or thirty years, the Mexican government at the higher levels was, in fact, significantly manned with what came to be known as "Gómez's boys." Among them, during most of the 1980s, were the president, the finance minister, and two heads of the central bank. And there is little doubt that the example of those highly competent and professional people had an influence on others far beyond their own numbers. To my mind, "Gómez's boys" and the Mexican central bank have been a significant reason Mexico has broken from the underdeveloped ranks to dynamic growth in a context of economic liberalism.

My second example is the Bank of Italy, a relatively new European central bank (it is less than a century old). The Bank of Italy is located in a country that, to put it kindly, has not been marked by great continuity in governmental leadership and a strong record of professionalism and integrity in governmental administration. Moreover, the Bank of Italy is an institution without a high degree of *formal* independence. While it exercises important authorities by law and tradition, decisions on monetary policy can be overridden and directed by the government.

Whatever the law, as a result of particular Italian circumstances and partly by drawing on central banking traditions, the Bank of Italy became a center of stability for economic policymaking in Italy. Whether or not there was a new prime minister every two or three years, whether or not Treasury ministers changed frequently, or whether or not the Parliament could meet legislative time tables, the central bank of Italy could act, could advise, and could maintain a certain consistency and coherence in coping with the difficulties and huge budget deficits, banking problems, and other matters.

Amid the turbulence of Italian politics, there is no doubt that the Bank has been considered a bastion of integrity and stability, providing a base for confidence that might have been otherwise lacking. For example, when Italy at times has had foreign payment problems and has needed some money from abroad in a hurry, that money could be obtained in large measure because foreign banks and governments had faith in the determination of the Bank of Italy to meet its obligations, and in the stability of the institution and its policies. That is the payoff from nurturing professionalism and continuity over long and difficult years.

Central Banking Is More than Monetary Policy

These two examples illustrate an important point: there is more to central banking than monetary policy. Some academic economists argue that you do not need the central bank—you can have a well-programmed computer that determines the appropriate money supply day by day and maintains a strict monetary rule better than people can, even if those people are removed from crass political pressures.

The policy problems the United States is facing in the early 1990s undermine that simplistic argument. Every day we can pick up the paper and read about whether banks are willing to lend, about bank failures and the savings and loan failures undermining the stability of the financial system, about concerns as to insurance companies; and mingled with it all, we receive sharply different "signals" from different measures of the "money supply." These issues have as much to do with a willingness to lend and people's ability to borrow, and the attitudes of savers, as with the technicalities of monetary policy. There are no set rules for dealing with such problems. The psychology of financial markets, and the state of financial institutions, is intimately connected with how the economy works. If you ignore that reality in conducting monetary policy, you will be making a mistake. In the real world, factors that may be difficult to identify or measure in academic work can make an enormous difference in how a policy works. These factors must be taken into account, and a central bank has a natural interest in doing so and in trying to deal with problems in advance, so that they do not become serious and undercut the objectives of economic policy. To do so effectively, a central bank needs competent professionals with exploring minds and the experience to deal with the problems.

Moreover, in dealing with these broader problems, a central bank must be involved in issues other than "monetary policy," narrowly defined. One can always debate whether the Federal Reserve, or other central banks, is doing as good a job as it should in banking regulation or in surveillance of the financial system; why the BCCI problem festered so long; what happened when Salomon Brothers repeatedly inflated bids for government securities; and so on. But, in my view, the Fed has done a highly credible job year in and year out—much better than other more politically oriented institutions without the tradition of professionalism would have done or could have done.

I believe that in order to be effective, central banks must have direct involvement with the important banking issues, such as mergers, banking powers, and deposit insurance, because the way those issues are resolved will, by affecting the institutional setting, importantly influence the stability, continuity, and effectiveness of financial markets. This is not to say that other arms of government should not also have direct involvement; it is only to say that the central bank should be one important element in the process.

Most central banks have broadly comparable powers; most central banks are to a greater or lesser degree involved in banking supervision and financial market supervision, and so they naturally become instruments for coordinating banking regulation, banking supervision, and banking structure. This is as it should be.

Central Banks and the Internationalization of Financial Markets

The ongoing internationalization of financial markets reinforces the need for central banks to be involved in a broad set of financial issues. It is hard to do anything these days without confronting some international dimension, and it is hard for anything really important to happen abroad without having some implications for our markets. Central banks, by tradition and necessity, are typically international and thus play an increasingly important role. Let us consider one of the international issues that is being addressed by central banks in the early 1990s—the question of the uniformity of bank capital requirements around the world. This question sounds simple, but, like many issues in financial regulation, it is not. While most people would agree conceptually that it is important to have a reasonably even and fair framework for competition among banks internationally, they do not agree on what is fair in practice. Moreover, every country likes to have control over its own destiny, but a country must give up autonomy if it agrees to an international standard. Then there are the difficult technical problems imposed by differing institutional practices. Formally equivalent stated capital requirements will sometimes result in different effective capital requirements. How do you put it all together in a sensible international standard? I would suggest that the international experience and responsibilities of central banks, together with their banking expertise, provide some of the essential ingredients for success.

Similar questions of international standards exist in other areas—investment banks and insurance are only two examples. These issues must be addressed in the 1990s, and central banking expertise will be a necessary component of that process, even if the decisions are made elsewhere.

Central Banking and Monetary Policy

I would like to conclude with a brief discussion of monetary policy, and how intellectual cycles influence the conduct of monetary policy. I am getting old enough to have lived through several swings of opinion about the role and effectiveness of monetary policy.

When I was at college, I wrote my senior thesis on the Federal Reserve. Those were the days when the Treasury bill rate was three-eighths of 1 percent, and the big issue was whether the Federal Reserve should maintain its policy of supporting a ceiling of 2.5 percent for long-term Treasury bonds. That low rate was a heritage of the 1930s depression, and was maintained during World War II.

At the time, the Federal Reserve was under Treasury (and presidential) influence, and it took a long time—really until 1951—for the Fed to retrieve its freedom of action and to cease the support of the bond market.

But, even then, there was a good deal of intellectual skepticism about the effectiveness of monetary policy in stabilizing or, even more importantly, influencing the economy. Monetary policy had been considered something of a failure in the 1930s, not so much because it was conducted incorrectly (that was a later view, popularized by Milton Friedman) but because it was not a very powerful instrument for controlling depression. Much of the emphasis, and the hope, was placed on the effective use of countercyclical fiscal policy, following the Keynesian revolution in policy thinking. Moreover, the view was popularized that a little inflation was a good thing, tending to make businesspeople and consumers optimistic and put them in a spending and investing mood.

The Rise and Fall of the Phillips Curve Trade-off

The view that a little inflation was a good thing became formalized in the so-called Phillips curve trade-off, suggesting inflation and unemployment were inversely correlated. For a while that statistical relationship seemed to hold. Then came the inevitable extension of thinking: If a little inflation helped reduce unemployment, then it should not be resisted. And if 1 or 2 percent inflation is acceptable, and even a good thing, it is not a great leap of analysis or faith to say that 3 or 4 percent is an acceptable price for a buoyant economy. People did not quite state it that way, but nonetheless I think this was the prevailing attitude among many influential economists, policymakers, and opinion leaders in the 1950s and 1960s.

I do not mean to say people in general were not concerned about inflation. Certainly, the Federal Reserve itself expressed a great deal of concern about inflation and at times, by the standards of the 1930s and 1940s, maintained quite restrictive policies. Nonetheless, powerful social and political pressures focused on reducing unemployment, even at the cost of some inflation. And for a while that approach seemed to work well. For a couple of decades, inflation remained limited, and the economy performed much better than it had before World War II. In fact, there was a period of sustained growth, interrupted only by short recessions, virtually unparalleled in our history. By the end of the 1960s, people had reason to feel pretty good about the conduct of economic policy.

In the 1970s, the situation began looking different. The inflation rate kept ratcheting up. The oil crisis and the sharp depreciation of the dollar in the early 1970s provided much of the impetus, but, in the absence of effective counteraction, higher rates of inflation became accepted as a part of economic life. However, as inflation became anticipated, the idea that you could "trade off" a little more inflation for a little more growth did not look so good: the inflation rate was running at 5, 6, 7 percent, and the growth rate was not doing so well. By the end of the decade, inflation was getting up into double digits and seemed to be accelerating. And, after a decade of slower growth and increasing financial instability, economists began to question the old dogma: inflation began to be associated with a sense of crisis, not prosperity.

I am not sure how far the change in thinking went among economists, but there is no doubt that among the public, the feeling of crisis about the high rate of inflation and the uncertainties associated with it began providing a political base for a stirring of economic policy generally, and for a strong monetary policy in particular—conducted by a politically independent Federal Reserve.

The resurgence of interest in greater price stability, tolerance for restrictive monetary policies, and respect for an independent central bank was reflected and even amplified in the rest of the world during the early 1980s. Now, more than ten years later, we are in quite a different psychological and political situation. In the 1990s it is again respectable to say that the first—and some people would say the only—job of the central bank is to maintain price stability.[2]

The New Price Stability Philosophy

The current prevailing wisdom is that reliance on a trade-off between unemployment and inflation was a great mistake—that the inverse correlation could not hold once inflation became anticipated. Now we hear the reverse of the earlier approach; we hear, "Let's get back to fundamentals and restore stability, and growth in the economy will take care of itself." In this new philosophy, the central bank has become a much more important institution because control of money is central to control of inflation.

In my environment, it has become respectable for the first time in my conscious lifetime to talk about amending the Federal Reserve Act to say the primary responsibility of the Federal Reserve is price stability. I strongly doubt that this will be a feasible legislative initiative for some time, but it is interesting that people in and out of the Federal Reserve are willing to raise the issue.

A more extreme manifestation of the philosophy is reflected in the Maastricht Treaty, providing for a common currency in the European Community and a new European central bank. The treaty simply states, "The objective of the European central bank is to maintain price stability," without qualification. And the treaty contemplates institutional arrangements that provide a very high degree of independence for the new central bank, should the common currency come into being. That independence could not be ended by any purely national law.

The new philosophy can also be seen in the Eastern European central banks now springing up. Their primary concern is with inflation, even as their economies experience unemployment rates over 20 percent. Even in Latin America price stability is becoming a central concern.[3]

The strength of the concern about inflation and stability, as compared to any other post-World War II period, is reflected in the fact that countries have been willing to tolerate much higher rates of unemployment. Germany sat through most of the decade of the 1980s with a very proud record on inflation, but 8 or 9 percent unemployment, and now, with the problem of reunification, is maintaining exceptionally tight money. The French place a very high priority on avoiding devaluation, and the British, while achieving much lower inflation, have had a long recession.

To my mind this change in philosophy reflects a growth in wisdom. I think central banks *ought* to be particularly concerned with price stability; I think that *over time* the economy will work better with price stability. No doubt, there is some inflation/unemployment trade-off in the short run, but that trade-off will not last if inflation becomes a way of life.

No doubt it is also true that we cannot be satisfied with chronically high rates of unemployment here or elsewhere. The implication is plain. For all the importance of central banking, money and finance is only one part of the economy and economic policy. There is obviously a great deal to be done in other areas, in government finance and elsewhere, to speed the return to a happy combination of growth and stability.

In that effort, government is going to have to restore a sense of trust in purpose and competence in action that is essential to the success of central banking. That, in turn, rests on the integrity, understanding, and dedication of a succession of human beings, up and down in the hierarchy—the very qualities that Alan Holmes brought to his years of public service.

Notes

1. All this was written before the election of President Clinton brought a new sense of anticipation and hope to many. It will be interesting to see if the renewed interest of some in public service will be maintained and will grow.

2. I say "again" because you really have to go back before World War II to find a comparable period.

3. In practice, Russia has become an exception, reflecting very different circumstances, but monetary policy has become the central issue in the reform agenda.

DENNIS WEATHERSTONE

Change and the Art of Monetary Policy

A key element in the art of monetary policy is coping with change. Change is going on all around us; the role of the Fed is to cope with that change as it fulfills its three primary missions: managing domestic monetary policy, regulating bank holding companies and banks, and serving as a lender of last resort for the banking system. In the 1990s the most important change that central banks will be facing is the globalization of monetary policy, so here I mainly discuss the problems central banks will have in coping with that change with reference to globalization of monetary policy.

Alternative Approaches to Change

There are many ways a central bank can carry out its mission. For example, the Fed has a formal structure while the Bank of England works more informally. Since most of this volume will focus on the Fed, let me add some perspective and briefly discuss the Bank of England before I specifically discuss the changes central banks must cope with as they deal with the ongoing globalization of monetary policy.

The Bank of England, which was founded in 1694, has 300 years of experience in being a central bank. It conducts regulatory policy in a flexible style; its powers are broad. The Bank of England is the banks' superviser for regulatory purposes. It takes care of monetary policy and the discount window; it mandates the foreign exchange policy; and it is also very much involved (in an indirect way) in the selection of key people at the various banks.

Because its officials mix freely with the banking community, the Bank of England traditionally has had superb knowledge of what is going on. In fact, the Bank of England used to run a few corporate accounts *at* the Bank of England deliberately so that its officials understood not only the banks, but the clients as well. They know what is going on because they are directly involved in those goings on.

I came to the United States in 1971 to run the foreign exchange and international money market business for Morgan. It was when the dollar was beginning to float. I thought, "Well, I'd better communicate"—as I had been used to communicating with the central bank (which, when I was in England, was only a short walk from where I worked). My initial question was, "Who knows whom?" I soon discovered an enormous difference between the Fed and the Bank of England.

My first sense of this difference came through a call from Arthur Burns, who was then chairman of the Fed. I did not know that he knew me. He said, "I would like you to send me a regular updated report on what's going on in the foreign exchange markets because we are floating and there is a lot of change going on." I thought it was strange that the chairman of the Fed should ask *me* for that. The Bank of England would *never* ask a person that, because *they* knew, much better than *we* knew. He then said he would like this updated report weekly. Well, reading a weekly report on the foreign exchange market is like reading yesterday's newspaper. After those requests I realized that the Fed's interest in foreign exchange markets was totally different from the Bank of England's. In 1971, foreign exchange developments were not important to the United States. These were things that other countries had to worry about. The United States did its business in dollars, and if other people had other currencies, and wanted them changed into dollars, that was their business.

I did this weekly report for about six weeks. Then one day I got a call from the New York Fed, and they said to me: "Well, we understand your bank is quite active, and you're doing a lot of arbitrage. Could you give us a weekly report on the foreign exchange market?" Once again I thought, "This is rather odd," and, showing my lack of knowledge of the U.S. system, I said, "But I already *do* that." That is when I discovered that the New York Fed was separate from the Washington Fed, and that they apparently did not talk to each other.

I am not being critical of the Fed. I do not think the foreign exchange markets were terribly important at that time. It is generally a mistake to make judgments about what is institutionally right or wrong. Different situations call for different institutions. My point is simply that there are many ways of operating a central bank, and those ways are built into the structure of the institutions.

It was not only the Fed that was different; Morgan-Britain was different from Morgan-U.S. At Morgan-U.S. we ran our foreign exchange activities quite separately from our domestic money market positions. In Morgan-Britain both were run by the same person, because interest rates and exchange rates moved in tandem. The prices of money, whether exchange rate price or interest rate price, were closely related to each other—so we managed them together. At Morgan in New York, and at the Fed, these functions were separate. Starting in 1976, that changed. The U.S. banks and the central bank began more closely integrating their foreign exchange and their monetary activities, although the responsibility is still separated.

A second difference in style between the Bank of England and the Fed consists of the formal structure of the rules. The Fed had a formal structure; the Bank of England did not. How did the Bank of England manage without so many rules? By the "eyebrow policy." If they did not like what you were doing, they would do the equivalent of raising their eyebrows. They would ring up and ask, "Would you like to come over for a cup of tea?" Such invitations were generally not good news. The rule of thumb for most banks was that they should get a cup-of-tea invitation about once a year. If they got it more often, they were probably doing something they should not be doing; if they did not get an invitation once a year, they were not showing enough independence.

These informal rules worked. For example, in the 1960s there were exchange controls in Britain. The government, trying to protect its reserves, had done a fairly good job of preventing currency from leaving the country. In order to hold foreign currency, banks had to get permission from the Bank of England. All payments and receipts of foreign currency were subject to Bank of England exchange control regulations. These controls included gold: since gold was freely traded around the world, it was treated as the equivalent of foreign currency. In our work we discovered that silver was missed out of the regulations. At that time silver played a similar role to gold, which presented us with a silver opportunity. We could stay within the regulations and get around the exchange controls. We could turn our domestic sterling into silver and then turn silver into foreign currency. With just some simple accounting techniques—with that loophole—we could have made a great deal of money.

I checked it out with the lawyers, and they said, "Absolutely fool-proof." I called my people in New York—because I was in London then—and said, "You know, this is what we can do—either here or in New York." We could have done it legally, but we could not have done it morally. And we did not do it. Instead, we went to the Bank of England and said, "We've found this huge loophole in the regulations here. Is it all right if we use it?"

Their answer was what we knew it was going to be: "Please don't do it, and we will fix it. We will change the law, but it will take us some while to change the law, and we'd appreciate it very much if you wouldn't do it."

In UK terms, that meant, "Don't do it." And we would not have *dreamed* of doing it, or telling anybody else, or finding out how to put it through an intermediary. You just would not think of doing that. The rules of the Bank of England at that time depended on the spirit of the regulation, not the letter. The Bank of England expected us to go beyond the letter. The system functioned really quite well. In the United States the situation was different. In the United States the rules go more by the letter, and both the Fed and the banks know it.

These examples are from the 1960s and 1970s. Since then, the Bank of England, through the growth of markets generally, has gotten more formal. England now has a separate securities board that regulates the securities market. For its part, the Fed has gotten more involved in the market and has established more informal communication, which increases the importance of the spirit, as opposed to the letter, of the rule. So globalization has brought the two regulatory systems together.

Coping with Change: The Blurring Lines Between Financial Institutions

A second area in which significant change is occurring is in the institutional structure of banking, as the business of banking has changed dramatically over the last ten or fifteen years.

Ten or fifteen years ago, it might have been generally correct to say banks' basic business was taking deposits and making loans. In the last fifteen years, there has been a melding of the roles of banks and securities firms in the United States. Banks today have active trading operations in all kinds of financial instruments. They do a lot of advisory work and much more underwriting of debt and, increasingly, equities.

Similarly, securities firms are doing much more of the business that was traditionally done by the banks. It is getting quite difficult to distinguish between the activities of so-called commercial banks and so-called investment banks. In fact, some banks today try not to designate themselves as either. Since banks are becoming like securities companies and securities companies are becoming like banks, the discount window should be available to investment banks and securities houses, not just to the banks. That, in effect, is happening already, but through an indirect route.

For example, consider J.P. Morgan. Internally, we talk about "the firm" more than "the bank." We see ourselves as simply providing financial services to our clients; when their needs change, the services that we provide change along with them. If we can not provide the services they need because the law will not let us, then we go down to Washington and batter on the doors and say, "We'd like some changes in the law." We do so not just to make more money, but in order to serve our clients better. This change in the structure of financial institutions will require a change in central bank regulatory attitudes. An example of the need for change can be seen in the stock market crash of 1987 and, earlier, in the silver crisis. In both of those cases the institutions that were hurt were the investment banks and the brokerage houses, but the implications were serious for the entire financial system. In response to these crises the Fed asked the banks, "Will you stop this from becoming a systemic problem? Lend these people money; don't cut back your lines just because you're worried that they may be hurt."

And so the banks responded. They helped the Fed during the silver crisis; they stopped a couple of brokerage houses from failing, and in October 1987, most banks—but not *all*, and this was interesting—kept their usual facilities available. They did not panic or cause a problem, so it worked out only because most banks did *not* follow their own self-interest.

At a Fed conference, I discussed the problem. My message to the Fed was:

> These days may be over. It was all right in 1987 and in the silver crisis, but investment banks and brokerage houses are increasingly doing the same kind of business that we do. They are active competitors, and in those crises you took care of my competitors with the

discount window when they got in trouble, not me. These competitors are clients as well, in that we lend them money. But with the growth of off-balance-sheet transactions, I can't go in and see what they're really doing, especially in a crisis—it's too complicated. I'm not their regulator, I'm not the CFTC, I'm not the SEC—I can't find everything out.

What *you* should do is just as you do with *us*: you come in, you examine us and the other banks so that we are comfortable when we deal with them. You're going to reach a crisis one day, and you're going to call us, only to hear, "*You're* the lender of last resort, not us, and we don't want to lend any more." We're not saying we're there *yet*, but you should *think* about that and change the discount window policy. It doesn't concern me from a competitive point of view. We can compete; we're not worried about that. So we recommend that you open the window to others, because otherwise if you get a crisis, and if the banks don't work with you, the crisis would be a major one.

That message was back in June 1989. As you know, the rules haven't changed, and we almost had the crisis with Drexel Burnham. That situation was difficult—more difficult than people knew. More recently, there was the problem with Salomon Brothers. That has been handled, but it is the kind of thing that worries me. There is a serious need to rethink the discount window in order to take into account what is going on in the markets.

Coping with Change: Arbitrage and the Derivatives Market

Let me now turn to an ongoing change with which the regulatory system has only begun to cope: the growth of derivatives and global arbitrage.

In the last few years, new financial instruments called derivatives have been developed. Derivatives started with swaps. In very simple terms, a swap is the exchange of obligations under one contract for obligations under another contract—the exchange of a risk you do not want for one you are more willing to accept. Swap obligations started out with interest rates, when some corporations decided that they would prefer a floating rate obligation on their debt, instead of which they had a fixed rate; and somebody else who had a floating rate wanted to have a fixed rate—so a market developed, a swap market, which put these two parties together. We managed a trade that allowed each to keep the same principal amount on the balance sheet but to swap the fixed and floating interest rates. That was the beginning of the swap market.

Swaps have developed enormously since then. Once people realized that they could be quite useful, the market expanded. Someone said, "Well, I have an obligation to pay Deutsche marks, but I'd really rather have the obligation to pay pounds, because the Deutsche mark looks as though it's getting strong and the pound looks as though it's getting weak. I'd like to do a swap on the currency." So the bank would find somebody else who had the opposite position and we would put them together. Currency swaps soon supplemented interest rate swaps.

In the 1990s, so many different types of swaps have developed that we need a generic name, derivatives, to describe the breaking up and swapping of the components of various obligations. A derivative contract simply means a contract that is derived from, or originated from, an underlying or basic contract. For instance, take the stock market, in which people deal in stocks and shares of a whole variety of different companies. The Dow Jones Index measures price movements in the market for thirty stocks. If you deal in the Dow Jones Index—buy it and sell it—that is dealing, in modern-day parlance, in a derivative. It is not dealing in the individual stocks themselves; it is in a derivative— an index derived from the combined prices of all these stocks.

Derivatives are useful. They provide methods of hedging, of offsetting risks, and of creating a financial portfolio tailor-made to your specific desires. Swapping derivatives is a form of arbitrage, and, like arbitrage, it starts out to serve a useful purpose—but we have to watch it in case it is abused.

Regulatory and Other Arbitrage

Another problem that central banks will be coping with in the 1990s concerns what I call regulatory arbitrage.

Most people, when they talk about arbitrage, think of foreign exchange because that is the oldest form of arbitrage: taking advantage of different prices for currency between one center and another—which is more difficult today because of technology, of course, as communication is practically instant. Arbitrage started with foreign exchange and then spread to interest rates, as people have arbitraged, say, Deutsche mark interest rates against Swiss franc interest rates.

Now we have arbitrage in regulations. In other words, if you see that it is easier to do a piece of business in Switzerland because of the regulations there than it is to do that same piece of business in London, you would consider choosing Switzerland. That is regulatory arbitrage. And then, there is tax arbitrage. When you borrow money or invest money, you not only look at the interest rate return and the foreign currency exposure; you want to look at the transaction after tax. So if you can find a place where the tax burden is reduced—looking at tax havens like Nassau or Luxembourg or other tax-hospitable countries— you get what I loosely describe as tax arbitrage.

Such arbitrages must be watched carefully because there are many temptations, and regulators of necessity are playing catch-up. For regulators do not *develop* these ideas and these products; they simply come along and supervise them after the fact. I believe it is part of my job to let them know what is going on so that they can be quick in getting up to date. This is self-interest, because if regulators are unaware and we get a systemic problem, it will affect all of us. It is no good saying, "Well, *I* don't do this sort of thing." If I've got some credit exposure to the guy over there, and *he* does it, then we both lose out.

Conclusion

There are, of course, many more areas in which change is occurring and modifying the role of central banks, but the ones I have discussed should give a sense of how important change is, and how important it is for central banks to keep up with, and even stay ahead of, those changes.

3

ROBERT C. HOLLAND

The Limitations of Monetary Policy

This essay is about the limitations of monetary policy. In choosing this topic, I recognize that, given the success of monetary policy in recent years, I may sound to you like the football coach who, after the team scores a big win, says, "The defense gave up 150 yards; we missed three big passes; we fumbled; two of our best players got hurt: we've got real shortcomings." But such cautionary notes are necessary.

Monetary policy is a powerful instrument that has come off a big win. Monetary policy scored at the end of the 1970s and in the 1980s. By taking the right steps, it stanched an inflation that looked unstanchable as the 1970s drew to a close. In the later 1980s, as people looked to macroeconomic policy to smooth out our economic ups and downs, the other major instrument of economic policy, fiscal policy, became so distended by a succession of deficits that it had virtually no flexibility left to inject some countercyclical impetus in economic policy.

Monetary policy became the only macro-instrument left in town with the leverage and ability to move and change. But monetary policy has not always been so dominant.

When you look back at our monetary history, you will see that, more often than not, our society was asking monetary policy, the central bank, to do things monetary policy could not do. Thus, a careful and realistic analysis of monetary policy and its structural limitations is necessary in order to decide what we should ask it to do and to prevent society from asking it to do more than it can.

There are three broad categories of limitations. The first is limitations in human capabilities—predilections, frailties. The second is structural limitations inherent in our central bank—how the Fed operates and what it operates on. The third is economic structural limitations—problems and shortfalls imposed by the basic economic structure.

Limitations in Human Capabilities

One simply need look at the newspaper to recognize that human frailty, human shortcomings, human mistakes, and human moral and ethical weaknesses are realities that allow bad things to happen. These problems are not new. For example, Adam Smith, the author of *The Wealth of Nations,* also wrote a book called *The Theory of Moral Sentiments*, which said for a free market system to work effectively there needs to be a grounding of moral and ethical standards in the participants in the market system. Without that grounding, markets will fail.

The problems of moral shortcomings can be epitomized in two categories: illegal greed and legal greed. Illegal greed in an affliction against which the central bank itself has no defense, as I see it. The only real defense is the law and the prosecutors going after whoever breaks the law and prosecuting them vigorously enough so that other would-be cheats and miscreants decide it is not worth the risk. Such actual or threatened criminal prosecution introduces questions of legal maneuvering, and other complexities. In the end, monetary policy has to operate with whatever people the law leaves in decision-making roles.

Legal greed is something different. It is unethical activity of one kind or another. The business of greed and selfish interest is both a virtue and a vice within Adam Smith's theory of the marketplace. It is the desire to earn that provides the incentive for a lot of market activity, but too much greed—greed that overrides the bounds that Adam Smith foresaw in his *Theory of Moral Sentiments*—weakens the system. In that event, then, you can have a potentially terrible shortfall. It is hard for us to imagine that taking place in this country. The last great shortfall occurred in the free banking era before the Civil War—more than a hundred years ago.

But over in Russia, events are taking place today that may give us an object lesson before long: a country is being broken apart, literally, by all kinds of shocks, with a currency system in which people are losing confidence. Rubles are being printed with nothing behind them. In that process, the integrity that makes money worth something may be lost entirely. If so, we will see both economic and personal tragedy result.

To see the importance of confidence, pull out a dollar bill from your pocket and ask, "What's that really worth?" Imagine trying to tell a Martian that that piece of paper is worth anything. He would not buy it. It is not even big enough for toilet paper, for heaven's sake. It does not have *any* value by itself. It is the integrity of the promise printed on it that counts. And if illegal greed, or legal greed, or any other human shortcoming undermines the public confidence in that piece of paper, then monetary policy (which works by leveraging the value of that piece of paper in the economy) loses its vigor. I hope the Russians do not give us as bad an example as I think they might. We will need to be watching them closely in the years ahead.

Our own central bank, the Fed, was designed by people who had a fairly lively sense that there were selfish interests around that might benefit themselves rather than others. As a consequence, the Federal Reserve System was constructed to include lots of checks and balances. Checks and balances are a traditional part of American citizenship and American government. The Fed was not designed until the early 1900s, and by that time there had been opportunity to learn from over a century's experience how the check-and-balance system was working in America. Consequently, one of the best check-and-balance systems was installed within the Fed, carefully designed to offset one selfish interest with another. James Madison would have been happy with the way that it was done. And that is no fluke, because the president who oversaw the creation of the Federal Reserve was also a first-class political scientist—Woodrow Wilson. The check-and-balance principle was very important to him.

On balance, the system has served our purposes well. Its designers did not get it perfect the first time. It needed some fixing in the mid-thirties, based upon the painful lessons of the twenties and the Great Depression, but it is still running today with plenty of checks and balances still in place.

Shortcomings in ethics and morals are one thing; shortcomings in brains are something else. This is another important limitation on monetary policy. The state of the art of monetary theory is not well even though monetary theory has done a lot of learning and growing and developing. Consider some of our past failings. We came out of World War I with a big, strong-looking, vigorous economic system and a monetary theory of how the banking system should create and back money and credit. That theory got us in a nasty inflation–recession in 1920–21. The monetary theory espoused by the most famous monetary theorists in the country was "Tie your monetary millions to short-term self-liquidating commercial paper." Unhappily, we found out in the inflation–recession of 1920–21 that such a monetary base can go up fast and go down fast.

We partially learned that lesson, but as the twenties went on, we built up such a speculative boom that the ensuing bust in 1929–33 turned out to be another terrible episode for monetary policy. Why? The monetary authorities were following what was, by common consent, the best monetary theory of the time. That theory did not have in it any Milton Friedman. It did not have in it any John Maynard Keynes. It did not have in it any Paul Samuelson, Art Okun, Bob Solow, or Will Baumol—all of whom have contributed important theoretical expansions of the dimensions of monetary policy and led us to conceive a much better, and more appropriately meshed, monetary policy today. But in 1929–30 such ideas did not exist. We had to ad-hoc it. Gradually, the monetary authorities broke away from those earlier central bank theories. In fact, the Fed seized upon the ideas of John Maynard Keynes about as quickly as any authority in this country did. Sometimes the Fed did not call it Keynesian, but that is what it was.

We slowly worked our way out of the Great Depression, and developed new theories as a result. Now, I suspect, most experts think we have a fairly comprehensive and well-rounded family of monetary theories to guide monetary policy. But I also suspect that one of these years another major economic problem will arise to plague us and we will discover that the prevailing monetary theory does not handle it well. At that point the central bank, relying on the existing economic theory, will probably have misdiagnosed the new problem and we will have another financial bubble or squeeze. We are not perfect theoretically.

I do not believe any one theory represents a useful working guide to monetary policy by itself. I regard even Milton Friedman's theory as being partially useful in the context of these other theories. I believe elements of all theories are a useful set of guides. Not lockstep rules—although that is the way Friedman would handle it—but a series of theoretical guides that warns you against problems, indicators that an artful central banker can look to for some guidance. It is not neat, but it is practical and pragmatic.

Traditionally, the Fed's safeguard has been a pragmatic willingness to move away from theory—even the generally accepted theory—when the market it is working with does not seem to be in accord with that theory. That kind of pragmatism, often wrapped in broad or vague-sounding statements, just feels its way along, perhaps testing some new theory experimentally or using some practical expedients, to see if it can achieve better results. That is a second-best state of affairs. But it is better than nothing.

There, in a few paragraphs, is my sense of the human limitation side that monetary policy has to work with, described in an American cultural context. We would use somewhat different language if we were trying to cover European monetary experience, or that of some other countries. But the truth is, there is a fair amount of commonality in this kind of problem. Human limitations touch central banks in every country.

In point of fact, we owe a real thank-you to Woodrow Wilson and the other designers of the original Federal Reserve. Our particular design of how a central bank should be set up has stood the test of time very well; and now that there is talk of setting up a central bank for Europe eventually, they are talking about a Fed of Europe. Europeans like the check-and-balance idea as the safest way to begin to centralize monetary power in the European Community when—if ever—they reach the point where they are willing to give up that degree of sovereignty. That is a tribute, I think, to the wisdom of the idea that a central bank in a democracy functions best with a number of different nodes, whether those be countries within the European Community, or states—or regions, as in our country.

Institutional Structural Limitations

The second set of limitations of monetary policy consists of the shortcomings or the peculiar features of the financial structure within which it operates.

Basically, monetary policy operates by either squeezing or enhancing the credit leverage available to those financial institutions that are required by law to maintain monetary reserves in fixed ratio to their deposits. That squeezing or enhancing process either imparts earnings or takes away earnings and imposes losses on the financial institutions that are subject to it. Today, in the United States, these institutions are the member commercial banks of the Federal Reserve System. That means those banks need a capital base big enough to withstand some cycles of earnings going down into losses and then back up (but not so huge a capital base that management does not have to worry no matter how much earnings fluctuate; there was a time when some Japanese banks seemed to be in that position). For our system to work well, our banks need to have a reasonable capital base, so that when a Fed-induced reserve squeeze comes on, the bankers feel that they had better gradually tighten up their own credit expansion. If banks have too small a capital base, they not only have difficulty dealing with the ups and downs of their earnings but also may fail to keep the confidence of their depositors that their funds will always be safe and readily available. In short, if the banking system does not have an adequate capital base, the whole transmission process for the tightening phase of flexible monetary policy can start to seize up.

We have had periods in our monetary history when that happened very seriously, particularly during some of the agricultural failures back in the early part of the century. We had it as late as in the thirties because of the size of the Great Depression. We have not seen it since then because we introduced a systemic invention to offset that risk—we invented the Federal Deposit Insurance Corporation, and the Federal Savings and Loan Insurance Corporation, to help cushion the damage that could come from failure of customer confidence in the ability of depository institutions' ability to pay on demand. But that risk is still there. The FDIC and the FSLIC are second-best solutions. They do not fix everything. We have realized that in the 1980s and in the 1990s, as we struggle with the fruits of the moral hazard that government deposit insurance created. By that I mean the temptation for some bankers to plunge into high-risk, high-yield lending and investing. To them it has seemed like a "heads I win, tails you lose" proposition. It looks as if we are going to work our way out of this banking mess, but at a very high cost.

Over in the S & L industry, the counterpart problem blew up into even greater dimensions. We are still trying to fight our way out of that debris so that institutions like the traditional savings and loan associations can exist again. But that is a very open question.

The S & L debacle represented a second kind of structural inefficiency in our financial system. S & Ls provide savers with instruments that possess some of the attributes of money, but outside the formal monetary policy network of reserves. Does money you put into an S & L remain money? Do you think your savings account in a savings and loan institution is money? Can you buy things with it just as much as if it were a deposit in a commercial bank or paper dollars in your pocket? A great many Americans thought the answer to these questions was "Yes" in the 1980s, and then later they were jolted to find out about a few institutional differences and a whole lot of inconveniences, even if an S & L were insured.

In truth, our financial system ground out a huge volume of near-monies during the 1980s. The main reason was that interest rate relationships had reached a stage where it became very profitable for more and more financial intermediaries to get into the act of creating near-monies. Not only did S & Ls do it, so did the money market funds, the credit unions, and even the insurance companies. They ingeniously designed their savings instruments to provide a kind of near-money liquidity, so that in many respects those instruments did some of the work of money.

Another thing this ballooning total of near-monies did was to make it harder to decide how much real money the system needed. Would you judge that all this near-money did the work of, say, one-third of the money? Did we therefore need one-third less of Milton Friedman's M_1? There was no theoretical formulation to let you find out a clear answer. The Fed had to feel its way through this confusing period, and it was tough going. It was indeed a limitation on monetary policy.

Furthermore, it was a limitation that figured at both ends of the credit cycle. In the golden days in the 1970s, when these near-money institutions were making big profits and growing fast, they were enhancing liquidity in the economy. Statistically, it manifested itself as an increase in the income velocity of M_1. And that was rather inflationary, in my view.

But when inflation reached double-digit proportions in the late 1970s, the Fed countered by vigorously tightening reserve availability in ways that seriously pinched the financial intermediaries. Hardest hit were those, such as S & Ls, that were operating essentially by borrowing short and lending long. When market yields climbed a lot higher than the yields on most of the assets these institutions held, we had the proximate cause of the S & L crisis.

One big result of that crisis was a disproportionate contraction of credit, focused essentially on the parts of the economy that had earlier been fueled by the expansive credits granted by these institutions. The real estate credit market suffered the most, both housing and commercial real estate, for it had been sustained more than any other area by earlier expansive credit. Therefore, it suffered a disproportionate impact from the credit restraint of the inflation-fighting period from 1979 into the 1980s, and boy, did those people know it! That was in the days when Paul Volcker was leading the Fed through that very tight anti-inflationary fight. He has some souvenirs of that fight, and he gave me one that I still keep at home. It is a plank about two feet long, mailed to him by the Home Builders of America, with little termites drawn all over it as if they were eating it all up, and every termite has the word "Volcker" written on it. They were sure who their enemy was: it was not the guys who made the bad loans to begin with; it was Volcker who turned the honey-money off, bringing in the period of tight credit.

It is worthwhile to see this episode in a longer-term context. All during the post–World War II era, the country was in a housing boom of one degree or another. During this era, every time the Fed moved to tighten credit to fight inflation, it bumped into this disproportionate impact on housing. All kinds of complaints came pounding in on the Fed, through Congress and through the administration, for hitting housing so hard. It meant, in effect, that in a political democracy like ours, there was a limit on how far money could be tightened by the central bank without generating so much political backlash that its tight money policy would be outlawed by something Congress or the administration would do. It was a constraint, and it kept the central bank from being quite as tight as it would have been wise for it to be. I did not think so at the time. I remember we thought we were being heroic by squeezing down with tight money, persevering in the face of strong complaints that were coming in from everywhere, from the White House to the country newspapers. In retrospect, however, when I look back, it would have been better if we had been a bit tighter a bit earlier. The country might have been better off in succeeding years.

Now one relatively new limitation on monetary policy has emerged for the United States. We have developed an increasingly global set of capital markets, with money increasingly able to move from one of the major financial markets to another around the world in response to interest rate differentials. In that process, we have evolved a different kind of disproportionate impact of tight money. Now it is not housing and real estate that get so disproportionately hard hit when the Federal Reserve really tries to tighten up money in this country; it is the exporters in this country who get most clobbered. Now when we try to tighten credit in this country, and interest rates rise as part of that process, that rise in interest rates tends to attract capital from overseas, as long as the fundamental financial and political structures are such that people overseas have confidence that they will get their money back. As those interest rates climb, both absolutely and in relation to rates in other major world markets, in comes capital from overseas; it comes in faster than our trade and current account balances can adjust, and therefore it drives the dollar exchange rate up. That increases the overseas prices on Chryslers and Fords and computers and everything else we were selling at prior exchange rate values, and starts pricing those U.S. products out of the world marketplace.

This happened drastically during the 1980s, for the first time in the post–World War II era. For a while, even smart CEOs in this country were a little puzzled about what was happening. I remember the head of Caterpillar Tractor coming in to see me. Caterpillar made the best heavy earth-moving equipment in the world, and had been selling a lot internationally. "What's hitting us? What's pushing up the exchange rate?" he kept asking. It was the rising exchange rate, elevated by heavy inflows of foreign capital, that was picking their pockets.

I must say that Caterpillar, and other major U.S. exporters, learned this lesson well. So did the Fed. Now this export vulnerability has become another practical restraint on how tight, relative to the rest of the major markets of the world, the United States can push its monetary policy. Tighten monetary policy and you clobber your export industries, and that is an important part of employment.

So we have another constraint: no longer just housing. This is because U.S. interest rates have not strengthened as much as in the past. Foreign capital inflows actually moderate the rise in U.S. interest rates, but push up our foreign exchange rate, which hits a different part of our economy. In effect, the disproportionate impact of tight money becomes distributed somewhat differently in our economy. As exports are hardest hit by a U.S. tight money policy, real estate is not hit quite as hard as before.

But however it is distributed, disproportionate impact of tight money is a *practical* constraint in a political democracy. Not only the Federal Reserve in this country, but central banks in other countries have found that too, to one degree or another.

I see a lot of different pressures that are pushing convergence and homogenization on the institutions within the financial structure. They are getting closer and closer to imitating one another; for example, they try to penetrate each other's markets. Most of these institutions were created in quite separate compartments for quite separate reasons. A whole variety of factors—competition, increased sophistication on the part of the average person in America, computerization (what electronics can do for you)—are driving these institutions closer and closer together. I would say there is a tremendous family of centripetal forces that are working to make these major financial institutions more and more alike as they try to compete more and more among themselves. That gets to the point of lender of last resort (access to which many investment banks want for themselves) because as these institutions become more and more alike, they need more of the same kind of support for safety's sake. The lender of last resort, which is so essential, I think, to the banking system, now becomes a little more important for some of these other institutions.

The key question, I think, is what is going to be the quid pro quo on the other side? What will be the quid pro quo to keep the kind of moral hazard from developing at the lender-of-last-resort window that we have seen develop with the deposit insurance corporations? What are the investment bankers advocating that the investment community give up, in terms of control? These investment bankers believe that because the Fed relies on the investment banks to get other financial institutions out of various binds, the investment banks have already rendered the service that should result in their being allowed access to the Fed as lender of last resort. But that should not be, unless there is a quid pro quo on the other side to cut down the social cost—that is, the social risk to the government of opening up that lender-of-last-resort function to those investment banks. The banks can see the additional benefit they would get from it; why do they not think about what is the quid pro quo that makes this a beneficial offer to society?

A quid pro quo—not necessarily the right one—might be the kind of rescue the Fed asked the investment banks to provide to the commercial banks during the October 1987 crash. But the point is that any access to the Fed lender-of-last-resort window ought to be accompanied by constraints on how, when, and where it could be used that would avoid this being a risk enhancement.

Right now my own private view is that there is a clause down in the bowels of the Federal Reserve Act that *would* allow a Federal Reserve Bank to lend to an investment bank if the situation should reach a point where at 4:30 on a Friday afternoon, Salomon Brothers—to take an example—calls up and says, "We've got perfectly good government securities for collateral, but we're a billion short of covering our settlements for the day, and that lousy bank of ours has just decided they won't give us any more credit." In that situation, the Fed could lend to Salomon Brothers.

But Federal Reserve officials do not talk about that much. The reason they do not talk about it is obvious when you stop to consider it. That particular clause was tucked into the Federal Reserve Act in the 1930s, when there *were* some problems of not being able to make payments. In effect, that clause is sort of the last resort of the lender of last resort.

I tend to sound like an old Scrooge, but, frankly, I think what we are going through is a massive transition in our economy that we need to go through. We need to squeeze down the unusually large share of GDP that went into consumer goods and real estate in the 1960s, 1970s, and increasingly in the 1980s. I think the share of our GDP that went to consumption and to domestic investment in real estate was too large for the long-term health of this economy. And I think that is why we ended up with some of the economic problems the Fed was facing in the 1980s.

Because of the excesses of earlier years, today we face a big budget deficit and a big foreign debt position. The way you fix these problems is to hold down domestic demand for consumption goods and for real estate, and try to expand the share of GDP that goes to exports—to goods and services that can be sold overseas. That, in time, redresses your trade balance, and creates a sounder income foundation for the economy. It is the kind of massive transition we are going through now. I think calling it a business cycle recession misses the larger economic purpose of the kind of transition we are in. Some of our citizens are being hurt in this process and they deserve some help, but the economy needs to be squeezed. We need more exports; we need more investment in productive facilities that enables us to increase exports, that creates the facilities in which we can make the kind of high-quality products and services we can sell in more places. That is the kind of adjustment that will give us a healthier economy tomorrow.

Economic Structural Limitations

The third category of limitations on monetary policy consists of short-comings in our basic economic structure that can interfere with the achievement of basic monetary goals. By the growth of economic understanding and the aspirations that have developed inside our country, we have evolved a fairly widespread governmental and public acceptance of three broad goals of monetary policy: holding down inflation, holding down unemployment, and promoting real economic growth—vigorous economic growth, some people would say; sustainable economic growth, other people that are of more prudential mind would say; but economic growth nonetheless. Three goals: hold down inflation, hold down unemployment, achieve good sustainable economic growth.

It is rare when an economy can achieve all three of those goals at the same time. Nevertheless, that does not deter some people who say, "These are the three things I'd like underneath my monetary Christmas tree. I want all three! Don't talk to me about trade-offs! I want all three!"

But the central bank has to live in a world of trade-offs, trade-offs imposed by some of the limitations I am talking about, that will not allow us to finance an economic climate that would achieve all three of those things at once. Such goals are particularly difficult to reach in concert if instead of saying "hold down inflation" you say "have zero inflation," which some people do say—even some Federal Reserve people. Or if you say, "My goal is not to hold down unemployment; I want zero unemployment. A job for everybody." A very laudable desire. People do better when they are working than when they are not working. Or if you say, "I want 5 percent real growth." That is a very vigorous pace. Striving for such extremely optimistic goals, however, lowers the chances of success.

In trying to hold inflation down, what you bump into are problems of inflationary ratchets and rigidities in many parts of our economy. The wage–price spiral was something we heard a lot about in earlier decades. We do not hear as much about it now, but it still exists, helping to hold up unemployment during this period of corporate restructuring and lay-offs. Cost-of-living escalator clauses have also become more pervasive. And once in a while we suffer inflationary shocks like the one we received from OPEC in the 1970s. All these things increase our inflation proclivity, and monetary policy cannot do much more than drag its heels. If it pushes harder to try to resist some of those inflationary proclivities, monetary policy then tends to slow down the rate of growth and push up the rate of unemployment, and bingo!, you get bad grades on goals two and three.

In the unemployment area, we have a family of problems that have ended up making an important share of the U.S. population not productively employable, at least not at the prevailing wage. And some of those problems come from surprising sources. I sometimes have asked, "What's the worst enemy of a successful low inflation/high employment monetary policy?" My brief answer: "The school system." A fuller answer would be, "The school system and the way we treat the children of disadvantaged people from the time they are conceived to the time they get into the work force." An important part of our population is not being trained in the skills necessary to perform the kind of work that needs to be performed in order to sell world-class products here and abroad.

What kind of future work force are we developing for our firms to employ? In this global economy, that is increasingly the yardstick we will be measured against. Can our producers utilize our future work force to turn out products of a quality and at a price that compete effectively with products coming from other producers in other countries? If they can not, their sales will flag and good jobs will start to disappear. What about the quarter of our children who do not get through high school? That share gets up to 40 percent in some major cities and within some ethnic groups. Those people are not employable in a world-class production facility. The last estimate of the National Association of Manufacturers was that nearly 40 percent of the age group of high school graduating seniors were not demonstrating in tests the kinds of proficiencies and skills that were needed to get meaningful jobs and succeed in business or in government or in industry. That is a terrible handicap for our society. The good news about this bad situation is that it is now widely recognized, and there are a lot of steps we can take to help remedy it.

The Committee for Economic Development, the organization I worked with during the last decade and a half, studied this area very carefully. It has produced a number of studies on the need to invest more in our children, to help disadvantaged young people learn, become educated, work better—to develop a new vision for child development and education that will make them more productive, more useful. This is good for them as individuals, good for society, and good for the economy. But it is going to take an estimated ten to twenty years at best to accomplish all this. And through those ten or twenty years, there is going to be an underclass in this economy that cannot cut it at the cutting edge that is needed in our most productive industries. This will be a first-class problem for society. It already is a nagging problem for the people running monetary policy in the central bank. The Federal Reserve cannot fix this underclass problem, but it can get blamed for the unemployment—or get harangued to make money much easier in order to push unemployment down, when in effect that would not reduce unemployment but would simply build up inflation.

The third goal our society has endorsed, a reasonable rate of economic growth in this country, is handicapped in an analogous way. Real growth in a country, we have learned now from the Bob Solows and Will Baumols of this world, comes basically from productivity, from learning how to make more efficient use of all the resources we can muster, working together. In contrast, the people who make up our unemployable underclass represent a positive drag on society. If you take all the students who drop out this year and you figure out how much more they would have made the rest of their lives in income and in production for the rest of society if they had stayed in school, the total adds up to roughly a quarter of a trillion dollars. Each year's drop-out crop is a lost quarter of a trillion dollars, in incomes for themselves and in goods and services for the rest of society. That is a terrible cost in forgone economic growth.

Conclusion

To sum up, if you look back over all three of the areas I have discussed and at the limitations in them, you are forced to conclude that monetary policy cannot do much to overcome those limitations. It is a mistake to ask monetary policy to try to fix them. But oftentimes our political system, or our citizenry, wanting something fixed and seeing nobody else fixing it, will ask monetary policy to fix it: "Jazz up the economy." "Lower the interest rate about another percent," says one of the CEOs at a business conference. "Give me about another percent lower interest rate." The interest rate is not what caused the trouble, but it is the fix the CEO can put a finger on.

We need to conceive the operational goals for monetary policy within the family of limitations I have talked about, and then work hard on the nonmonetary tools to shrink or fix those limitations. One good remedial tool is the kind of education reform that the Committee for Economic Development advocates. Another is improving worker training. A third may be redesigning welfare along the lines the Swedes developed, which allowed them to run an unemployment rate one-third as high as ours and still not suffer more inflationary kick out of that than we seem to be getting out of our system.

One monetary official who I think well understood these limitations of monetary policy was Alan Holmes. More than any other single person during the decade he headed the Federal Open Money Desk, Alan was the Fed official with his hand on the throttle of monetary policy push and his foot on the brake of monetary policy prudence. I never saw him when I thought he was entranced with that power, captivated by it, or being used by it. He had a very lively sense of the limitations on the power. But the true power, he did have. I had a job for about ten years at the Federal Reserve Board in Washington that put me on the other end of each morning's telephone call from the Federal Open Market Desk in New York. It was a joy to have a person like Alan making that call. He was a superb public servant—and all of us who knew him can be proud of him. As long as the Federal Reserve can attract and retain key officials as good as Alan Holmes, I think our monetary policy will be in pretty good hands.

That brings us all the way back to where we started—to the human dimension of monetary policy. And I am glad to end on a happy note: there are human beings who do things more right than the average, and when the central bank can have them in its employ, we are all better off.

4

Albert M. Wojnilower

A Primer on the U.S. Banking Situation

A banking system able to share risk is critical to the progress of the private sector, and hence to economic growth. Because of the failure to regulate our financial institutions properly, we in the United States have undermined the ability of our banking system to support and foster the development of novel or unstandardized—in short, risky— private enterprises. This means that economic development will be slowed and that future generations will be disadvantaged.

The Historical Background

The technological changes in the financial sector have been enormous. When I was a freshman at Columbia in 1947, I was the only one in my economics class who knew what a checking account was. Today, almost every student has a checking account and probably a credit card, too. Credit cards, except of a specialized sort, were unheard of as little as twenty-five years ago.

Checking accounts, credit cards, and many other technological advances have had enormous effects on what types of financial institutions make sense and are efficient, and on the appropriate regulatory environment. Regulatory change has not kept up with technical change, and its failure to keep up is, in many ways, responsible for the current sorry state of banking.

Our current regulations developed when people had to carry cash. Before credit cards and personal checking accounts, it made sense to have a multitude of financial institutions, operating mostly very locally. Legislation encouraged two or three competing banks in each local area. In the United States cultural framework, which has always been suspicious of the power of money and monopoly, it was natural to have regulations that assured active local competition.

But when people got cars and telephones, they ceased to be dependent on nearby banks. Indeed, once people got used to doing business by check, geographic proximity of the bank hardly mattered at all, with the result that there were too many institutions to remain profitable.

Our current regulatory structure can only be understood within this historical background. Because of political forces, a complex set of protective regulations developed which enabled the overpopulation of local banks to survive. One major restriction is that banks generally are not allowed to branch out of state. A minor but revealing requirement explains why, in most big cities, one actually sees so many bank branches. It is because of laws stipulating that bank branches have to have street-level entrances. There are myriad rules of this sort.

More anticompetitive regulations were spawned by the Depression. The most important were limitations on the interest rates allowed to be paid on deposits. Banks and thrifts were no longer free to compete with one another by paying higher interest rates: everyone was held to the same low maximum rate established by the Federal Reserve and other supervisory authorities. Together with the introduction of deposit insurance, at about the same time, this made each bank identical to every other from the standpoint of small depositors. One did not have to ask whether the bank was sound or not, or what rate it paid, because the deposits were federally insured and the rates were the same everywhere.

For decades, this was the environment in which our depository institutions operated. The system operated reasonably well until the 1970s.

But it was undermined by new technology. Finance became national and international, rather than local. The electronic technology that created automatic teller machines and credit cards also made it possible to assemble various kinds of loans that can be standardized into bulk packages salable as securities on the open market. As a result of this "securitization," local money no longer finances local mortgages or auto loans. When you borrow from the bank to buy a car or take out a mortgage for your home, the institution that decides whether you qualify and gives you the check generally is no longer actually lending you the money. Instead, it is in effect a packager for security dealers that sell securitized loans to investors from all over the world. Furthermore, securities such as stocks or bonds generally are no longer physically traded. They are computer book entries. Not having to transfer physical certificates from one place to another has made securities trading much faster and cheaper.

But what about loans that involve novel or risky ventures that cannot be standardized into securitizable form? That is the sort of lending that banks used to specialize in, particularly for smaller, not widely known companies. However, as banks fail and are otherwise constrained by new regulations designed to inhibit risk taking, many important banks have in effect left the lending business altogether. While other institutions may be evolving to take their place, it will be many years before the gap is effectively filled.

Another burden banks bear is that, in return for having originally been granted a monopoly on the checking account business, they are obliged to incur certain kinds of expenditures and meet certain rules. The monopoly has eroded, but the costs remain. Consider, for example, the checkable money market and bond funds. Such balances are not legally insured, but as a practical matter the giant funds are just as insured as banks, since the authorities cannot afford to risk the domino effects of a failure. The check you write on a money market fund, to be sure, is actually written on the fund's bank account, but the bank is only involved as a mechanical agent for which it earns a very small fee. This fee is a lot less than the bank would earn if the funds were deposited with and reinvested by the bank for its own account. But how can the money market fund pay higher interest than the bank? Because it does not have to pay deposit insurance premiums or maintain non–interest bearing reserves with the Federal Reserve. And because it does not have to have local offices open to the public on the ground floor or any other specific place. Its working headquarters can be in North Dakota.

Deregulating the Financial Zoo

Until recently our financial system resembled a rather neat zoo in which each institution operated in a nice cage, protected from the other animals and from the public, with nice keepers who made sure that the animals never died from disease or starvation. Each cage had a label designating the particular financial animal, what business it specialized in, at what prices, and in what geographical habitat.

As the technological obsolescence of this compartmentalized system became evident, the pressure mounted for deregulating and modernizing it. That is what was done during the 1970s and 1980s, but it was done thoughtlessly and recklessly. The chief tool of deregulation was to remove the controls on the interest rates payable to depositors. Suddenly all institutions, large and small, could offer high rates and attract funds from anywhere in the world. What each institution had to do was figure out how to invest the funds profitably, just when everyone else was trying to do the same in fields in which they had little or no experience. With institutions having to pay much higher rates and searching for new lending outlets in competition with one another, a tremendous squeeze developed on profit margins.

The natural consequence of knocking down the barriers among the animals in the zoo was to make each animal, unexpectedly, both predator and prey. The only way for individual institutions to preserve themselves and their employees was vastly to increase the volume of deposit taking and lending, to make up for the reduced profit margins with ever bigger volume. Suddenly, what had been a genteel, high markup "boutique" business became a supermarket.

With most banks eager and even desperate to make loans, it was inevitable that many bad loans would be made. Bad loans are those that, one finds out later, do not repay. In principle, the markups should have been larger than before, to compensate for the higher risks, but in fact the new competition made them much smaller. We were headed for the wholesale failure of financial institutions, when the authorities belatedly realized that this was intolerable—because so many of the deposits were government-insured and because losses on the other insured deposits would have produced general financial and economic paralysis.

The most extreme and widely publicized example occurred in the Savings and Loan industry. Actually, the government officials who planned and instituted deregulation—in both Democratic and Republican administrations—fully expected that Savings and Loans would disappear as a result. They welcomed this because of their belief that specialized financial institutions were obsolete.

But when the Savings and Loans did face wholesale failure in the early 1980s, the debacle was viewed as politically unacceptable. In response, all sorts of legislative, regulatory, and political changes were instituted that in effect told the Savings and Loans: "Play double or nothing. Take more chances. Make loans you didn't make before. We're changing your accounting so as to be much more generous in what we recognize as earnings." The effect was exactly what was to be expected. The losses mounted, not only at Savings and Loans but also at other lenders forced by competition to follow suit. The deposit insurance bills now being paid are a large multiple of what they would have been had the problem been confronted in the early 1980s.

In the commercial banking field, the same set of forces was operative, but the details were different. The commercial banks found one outlet in making huge quantities of loans to governmental organizations in underdeveloped countries, notably in Latin America. In this they were tacitly encouraged by our government, which viewed the loans as politically helpful.

When these loans soured, the banks (along with many insurance companies) turned to real estate lending, with disastrous consequences, especially in New England. A third major outlet was lending to support so-called "highly leveraged transactions." You have probably heard of junk bonds. Virtually all the junk bond deals depended on a huge volume of underlying bank loans. The attraction of the loans was precisely that they were enormous. If suddenly you need to increase lending by a huge multiple in order to maintain earnings, just when everybody else is trying to do the same, there is a great premium for thinking big. That is how these highly leveraged transaction schemes came to be generated. Desperate competitors were vying with one another to make the biggest loans on the riskiest projects, because those projects pay the highest rates. Any reasonable person could see the reckoning that was to come.

The regulatory reaction to these commercial bank loans differed from the Savings and Loan case. As mentioned earlier, the politicians and the supervisory authorities in effect combined to exacerbate the Savings and Loan disaster. In commercial banking, on the other hand, the authorities actively questioned many of these activities, but were ignored. The political and academic climate of the time was opposed to supervision in principle, because private decision makers were presumed always to have better judgment than government officials. Of course, when the problems finally boiled over, the politicians and public tried to make the examiners and supervisors the scapegoats.

This led to what I call the "revenge of the supervisors." It took various forms. Supervisors were now in a position to call the shots and became zealots in forcing banks to retrench. The Federal Reserve took the lead in persuading the banking authorities of other major countries, through the International (Basle) Banking Accord of 1988, to adopt strict international rules that require banks to maintain certain proportions of capital, based on the riskiness of their loans and investments. Here at home, the authorities, partly under the prodding of Congress, enforced standards that were much harsher still, and strong-armed banks and thrifts into shrinking themselves.

Appropriate as these new rules might be in principle, imposing them all at once on an overextended banking system had an effect similar to an increase in reserve requirements. Banks needed more capital. The only way to raise capital in a hurry is to sell stock to the public. But an industry with too many banks and bad loans will not be able to sell much stock. So, instead the banks had to improve their capital ratios by reducing their assets; that is, by calling in their loans and not making new ones. This has been exerting a pervasive contractionary impact on the economy.

Were this still the world of forty years ago or earlier, we would be in truly desperate economic straits, because banks in those times dominated the financial universe. In the meantime, however, banks have shrunk dramatically relative to other financial mechanisms, especially finance companies, mutual funds, and the securities markets. As a result, the lingering bank credit blockage impinges mainly on smaller, local, and new businesses. But this is still a very serious gap. Huge numbers of jobs are being eliminated in the military-industrial complex and other large organizations, and they can only be restored in new ventures—which these days, from a credit standpoint, are homeless.

Banking Is a Public Utility

Even if we were not burdened by these financial problems from the past, even if we were able to construct from scratch a new financial system, banking would still need to be a regulated system. If we want to continue to have the ability to prevent inflation and boom–bust cycles, we must have the means to limit the growth of financial institutions at critical times. Money and credit cannot be allowed for long to grow faster than the economy, or inflation will result. Nonfinancial industries are not constrained in this way, nor do they need to be. But because their growth is not capped, they are better placed than financial institutions to raise capital.

Furthermore, we have to assure the integrity of our payments system, which consists of those institutions on which checks can be written and the interconnections among them. The participating institutions necessarily have to be limited to those willing to accept certain rules that impose costs, but these costs are not inflicted on others. This means that the payments-system members are competitively disadvantaged relative to other institutions that benefit from the payments system but have not accepted expensive constraints. Again, the core financial institutions are rendered uncompetitive.

The social compact under which modern democracies operate is one that requires the core financial institutions to be a kind of regulated public utility. Without special protection, they would face a chronic threat of competitive failure. This, you will not be surprised to hear, is a highly controversial view, although not so controversial as it was ten or twelve years ago when I began to raise these issues in public.

The United States and other English-speaking countries adhere ideologically to a market system that can be characterized as one of "open outcry." Everyone publicly shouts his or her price, and the best seller and the best buyer consummate the transaction. It is all out in the open, visible to friend and foe alike.

This system has obvious virtues, but it also has its disadvantages. Be that as it may, it is quite different from most of the rest of the world. Elsewhere, banks and their business customers work together behind the scenes, and often the government is also part of the equation. In the United States the borrower's objective is to persuade (fool?) the lender into providing the largest loan at the lowest price. The lender's job is to investigate whether the borrower is telling the truth and later to monitor the borrower to make sure the borrower lives up to his or her promises. The relationship is adversarial: increasingly, borrowers are trying to find legal dodges for failing to repay even when they have the money.

This is not typical of other countries where relationships tend to be more cooperative and reciprocal, involving long-lasting interconnections and alliances. This produces strong tendencies toward monopoly and market rigging, and makes it hard for unaffiliated newcomers to enter the market. Such alliances may dictate terms to vendors and suppliers. But they will also take care not to drive them out of business so long as they perform well under circumstances that inevitably change in ways that no formal contractual agreement can anticipate.

We need to be aware that our system is not the only possible approach. It is not certain that it has been the better one. Even if it is, we might nevertheless find ourselves obliged to modify it in a world in which we compete with others whom we no longer can compel to do things our way. Let me urge you, then, to think of our banking problem as not essentially financial, but rather as a particular manifestation of an awesome challenge that all the world now faces: how to mobilize, in a modern sociopolitical setting, the strengths of both competition and cooperation, despite the propensity of each to destroy the other.

5

John Rau

Outlook for the Banking and Financial System: The Year 2000

The year 2000 will be marked by enormous structural and technical changes in banking both domestically and globally. Almost all the current U.S. restrictions on the banking industry that are based on geography—where you can bank, where your head offices are, how many states you can operate in—and functional restrictions, such as whether you can mix banking and investment banking, and even banking and commerce, will become irrelevant. If regulatory reform does not keep up with these changes, we will end up with a system that cannot compete internationally, and the U.S. banking system will lose market share. Either we keep up, or we lose out. There are no other choices.

The year 2000 will be characterized by enormous consolidation of the banking industry, but simultaneously with that consolidation, an unbundling of the services that banks offer. Consider some of the realities that we must face: In the year 2000 the average age in the United States will be forty-five. Twenty percent of the work force will probably be working at home. The United States will have a severe shortage of skilled workers. There will be a big shortage, not in the managerial senior executive sector, but in the knowledge and applied information systems sector. All of these will be major factors in the structure of the banking industry in the year 2000.

Each of the consolidation problems will require major changes in the structure of banking. Currently we have a system that delivers the service of banking by putting a small building with a bathroom someplace where people pass by. That is the basic technology today. Between now and the year 2000, more and more people will be working at home. As that happens, optimal location of banks will change from their current location.

Another change will be technological. By the year 2000, increasingly more homes will be geared up for the delivery of financial services, so the technology that banks use to deliver services will be radically different. When we look back we will say, "The 1990s is the decade when the world got united and the international banking rules were integrated." To facilitate this technical change, reciprocal licensing will become widespread. The current regulatory atmosphere is enormously deficient in cross-border regulation. One of the reasons that we had the problems with BCCI was that BCCI was able to exploit regulatory differences. It had its headquarters in countries that were particularly lax in financial regulation. Because the financial system regulation was conducted country by country, BCCI's activities went essentially unregulated. Clearly, this problem of intercountry regulation must be addressed. Unfortunately, it will only get addressed after a series of crises like BCCI cause some people to lose a lot of money.

The Push for Consolidation

In 1986 there were about 11,000 banks in the United States. In 1992 there were about 9,500. In the last five years, we have had 15 percent shrinkage in the number of institutions in this country. About 250 of those 1,500 banks that disappeared over this period died. The rest of them are floating around under a different name, and most likely as part of a regional or super-regional bank. This trend will continue through the 1990s.

Stakeout, Breakout, and Shakeout

There are three quite separate stages of the consolidation movement: stakeout, breakout, and shakeout. They occur in a predictable sequence. The first stage is stakeout. It consists of acquisition to obtain initial market entry. Generally, the acquired firm is small compared to the buyer, and the price that is paid incorporates a relatively high premium. That led me to invent what I call the FOBO rule if you are the seller of a bank. FOBO means, "First out, best out." Once the dust settled, there was a lot of evidence that the first sellers got the best premium. What motivated the buyer to pay a premium? Being first. "I'm going to have my flag planted in this state before anyone else." The driver was not economic. It was the equivalent of "Let's get to the North Pole" or "We'll have a man on the moon in three years."

The stakeout phase usually takes a year. Then it moves into breakout. That is where successful acquirers on a programmatic basis view acquisitions as a way of changing their scale. Their focus is on increasing their market share, which requires them to increase their profile in certain lines of business. The focus of these deals is not to plant the flag, but is, instead, synergy. The banks ask questions like "How do we fit?" in terms of market share, and there are clear economic goals that the deals must meet. Typically, if you were to ask a bank CEO who is an acquirer what are his or her criteria for doing these kinds of deals, you would find they are economic, dictated by the stock market. The market will punish the stocks of any acquirer that takes meaningful dilution. Banks have limits at this stage because if they cannot acquire a company in a way that does not depress their own earnings, they cannot just keep going. The market becomes a major check on expansion.

Most regions of the country, except the Midwest, are at the breakout stage. They have been through it in New England, in the Southeast, and in the Southwest. By the year 2000 the Midwest will have been through it too.

The third stage is called shakeout. Unlike the first two, shakeout is seller-driven. In shakeout, acquirers bottom-fish for bargains—banks that have gotten into trouble and need assistance. Shakeout deals are very opportunistic, as opposed to being either strategic or strategic/financial like deals in the first two phases.

Efficiency and Consolidation

The underlying force in the ongoing consolidation will be efficiency. As technology changes, so does the efficient market structure. The regulatory structure will have to follow the changing senses of efficiency.

Today, the rules that determine where banks can buy other banks and where they can operate are highly restrictive and geographically based. The basic rule is still: a bank can operate within a home state and in some states that touch its state. These rules will be significantly loosened by the year 2000. The push for consolidation will come from demographic and technological factors.

Efficiency is guided by banks finding their natural markets. One major driving factor in determining natural market is advertising costs. It costs a fixed amount to advertise to a certain market that is covered by TV, and you can reach all of the people in that market for the same cost. Once you pass into the next TV market, your costs step way up. So as the regional compacts give way, one will see increasingly that banks will start to say, "What is the natural market within which I can get some synergies by acquiring?"

Ultimately, natural market will be determined by the economics of the bank's operation. One of the key issues is that if you are going to acquire somebody in your market and pay a big premium, how do you get that premium back? A bank must find opportunities to do the same amount of revenue-generating work with less expense. And one of the biggest areas in which you can save is the operating units. If you can combine two back rooms and serve twice the volume at the original cost, you can pay the premium. Check processing centers and things like that can serve a certain physical region, but once you go beyond that region, you lose some of that margin. But this boundary of the economic zone of an operations center is moving outward with new technology.

What makes it so hard to determine natural market is that technology is changing. Technology is going to change the boundaries of that operations center. Many financial transactions take place other than by check. One of the biggest technical changes that is currently taking place concerns verification of transactions. Right now the market demands that banks save all that paper so that they can get it back to the customer—so the bank can, at the end of the month, say: "Here are your canceled checks." If banks could throw the paper away the first time it entered the system, there would be enormous cost savings. Why do banks have to keep the paper? Because customers want it back so that they can be certain they really wrote that check. If banks can convince customers that this paper trail is not needed, they can save money. It can, and will, be done. Look at the American Express card. Does American Express send you back the actual slip any more? No. They send you an image. We are getting to where when that check first comes in the bank can record the image. That is, the bank can digitize everything on it. Then when your statement comes out, if it is the cheaper model you just get a line description; if it is the expensive model, you will get a reassembled picture of your check. Everything will be digitized and available on line. Will that be OK for you, or do you really want the piece of paper?

Market research indicates that most people will be more than satisfied with the image. As the technology gets to where we can record all that data—all of this is driven by the price of technology—capturing it and sending it to the customer will require a relatively short string of data. The picture of your check is more complicated. It has to have a bit of data for every tiny square on the checkbook. In order to do that, the cost of shipping big numbers of bits has to come down to nothing. We are headed in that direction. Technology is ultimately going to eliminate most of the regional dimensions other than the marketing side.

Do Acquisitions Pay?

To say that there will be one enormous push for consolidation is not to say that on average the consolidations will pay off. They probably will not. About two years ago the Bank Administration Institute commissioned a company called First Manhattan Capital Group to do a strategic study of the success of acquirers and to look for the characteristics that distinguish successful acquirers. They studied twenty-six large banks known as vultures, going back to 1982. The vultures were those banks that in each year of the study added at least 10 percent to their equity in the form of equity to do acquisitions. They were active acquirers. At the end of the period, for twelve banks (called the "turkeys") it was clear that the effect of their policies of acquiring had at least somewhat reduced the value of their franchise. Only six were "eagles." These banks were worth more than they would have been had they not done anything. And eight of the twenty-six were "dead ducks"—it was clear that their acquisitions directly led to their either failing or becoming "distressed" acquisitions with major declines in shareholder value.

That conclusion about acquisitions is not unique to banks. It is pretty much the same in other industries. Acquisition as a strategy has no more than a 50 percent chance of succeeding at best. That does not deter people from doing it.

Another force toward consolidation will be globalization. In the year 2000 global nonbank competitors will be much stronger. Look at what has happened to commercial banks in the last ten years in terms of their share of total financial assets in this country. They have lost 20 percent of their relative share. To whom? To financial institutions in unregulated sectors and to foreign competitors. When I say globalization, I mean it in terms of both geography and global competition from institutions of all types.

Service Segmentation

While banks may not do too well in the year 2000, some financial institutions will, and that success will cause banks to modify their structure. One type of company that will do well is the financial information service company, like Dun and Bradstreet. It has a data base and credit ratings, and has made that a business, similar to credit bureaus and businesses of that kind.

A second type of company that will do well in the year 2000 is the type that sells computer services. Most banks do not develop their own computer systems. There are, however, companies that do their own computer work that are world-class in their niche.

Niche banks are going to have to think about how they can do well within their lines of service. Banks will have to start unbundling services, eliminating those they do not handle well. Consumers want to pick the best of each type of service. So banks are going to start identifying those activities that are not critical to their value-added. Take something like messenger services. Is it likely that there are 9,500 banks that are all good at messenger services? Individual banks need to find out what it is they are good at and then put their people and their focus there. If they themselves need other services, they can contract them out to other firms like IBM.

Up until now the idea has been that if you get bigger, and centralize everything, that will be more efficient. Jam it all into one big service operation. When you centralize stuff, although there are some economies of scale, you lose a lot because now nobody is really paying for it. The amount of influence and supervision you can exert over centralized management is minimal. The central people have multiple masters, and if they have multiple masters, they have none.

Centralized operations are going to be broken up. The model that the banks will use will be control over the fewest resources that the banks need to be efficient. Most people have had the experience of going into a bank and being told where to stand and what to do. The bank has been able to get away with forcing you to conform to its organizational structure. The teller can say, "No, no; you don't do that at this window. That's done at that window over there." In a globally competitive world where the customer has choices, the bank is going to shape itself to what the customer wants.

The key question in this country is: will our regulators let the risk-based system be the determining constraint? If they do, you will see more institutions going to specialized forms. Some will become high-capital, high-risk kinds of institutions; others low-capital, low-risk institutions. If they do not, if they hold to their paradigm, which is basically that most banks will have to have a certain amount of leverage or, as the British call it, gearing ratio, then I think that will lead to the demise of more small banks, because they will not be able to specialize and compete.

A word about legislation. The Treasury has put in a bill that basically says you have got to free up the banks from all these archaic proscriptions so that they can earn more money and be competitive on a worldwide basis. Therefore, you have to allow them to branch nationally; you have to eliminate Glass-Steagall, the barrier between banking and investment banking; you ought to move toward national regulation so that as opposed to having all this mishmash within a financial holding company, all the securities business would be regulated by the SEC, and all the deposit-taking business by the banking regulators. You ought to recapitalize the bank insurance fund. The Treasury has also proposed eliminating the barriers preventing industrial companies from owning banks. The industry generally supports such elimination of barriers as positive thinking.

But there will almost certainly be no change in the rule about industrial ownership—we will keep banking and commerce separate. We will probably nominally eliminate Glass-Steagall, but there will be such high firewalls, restrictions on what a banking company can do in the securities business with a customer who is common to both the banking and securities affiliates, that customers will still have to pick between one business or the other. Really, we will not get much mixing because of the politics of power and the securities industry. There will be no regulatory simplification. The politics of getting the Federal Reserve and the Comptroller and the SEC and the state banks to agree that any of them should sacrifice their bureaucratic roles in the cause of regulatory simplification just will not happen. The bullet will be passed around the table, and they will all say, "No, we should keep studying this." There will be no real reform of the deposit insurance system, which means that some of the temptations to excess that exist within it will continue to exist. We will still find banks getting into trouble. There will be some, albeit minor, reform of TBTF—Too Big To Fail. The implication of that is that even uninsured deposits are protected. No one is seriously arguing that the system should not have that flexibility. The argument is: why should the banking insurance fund have to pay the tab when some guy at the FDIC or the Fed decides that it is too big a risk to let, say, Chase Manhattan, go? The argument is not whether to pay, but who should pay. Should it be bank depositors, or should it be taxpayers at large?

Conclusion

Looking back from the year 2000, what will we have done? We will certainly have fewer banks and they will certainly be bigger. The successful banks will be the ones who are able to react fast. The market will automatically adjust long before the guys at the top make a decision and pass it on down the line. Strategies will be more focused on function and linkages to the market than on geography. But most important, the rule of the world is that there are no consolation prizes. If you are not one of the three or four best in the world in the thing that you do in your market niche, you will go under. And that is a whole different kind of world than today.

Part II

Real-World Policy

6

BRUCE K. MACLAURY

The Fed: Reconciling Autonomy and Democracy

Central banks are controversial and often unpopular institutions in most societies in which they operate. They are controversial and unpopular, I think, for four reasons. The first is that they have great power. They can make or break economic activity in a society—which is about as great a power as one can have.[1] The fact that central banks have great power means that they are political institutions whether they like it or not. Any institution in society that has power is going to be controversial.

A second reason they are unpopular is that they have an unpopular task to perform. They are the constituency established in American society to be the pleader and actor on behalf of "sound money"—that is to say, anti-inflation measures. Assuring the soundness of the nation's currency is one of their legislative mandates; that means preventing inflation from eroding the value of the dollar. Bill Martin, one of the great chairmen of the Federal Reserve System, used to say that the job of the Federal Reserve was to take away the punchbowl just as the party was really getting under way. In other words, once the economy is really getting up a head of steam, the Federal Reserve's assigned role is to step on the brakes in order to prevent the growth of the economy from getting beyond the capacity of production. The only question is: how hard?

A third reason central banks are controversial and unpopular is that the language and the institutional arrangements of the Fed are arcane, not easily comprehended by the person in the street who has to cast a vote. To most people, the Fed is a distant power headquartered in Washington, a Washington institution that speaks its own language.

A fourth reason concerns accountability. To whom, or to what institutions in a democracy, is a central bank accountable? Is it responsible to the administration? Is it responsible to the Congress? Is it responsible to the people? And, if it is responsible to one or more of these bodies, in what ways and how? The issue of accountability is probably the diciest political issue with which the central bank must wrestle. One reads about this accountability in the daily newspapers; about how the president of the United States, wishing to assure his reelection, wants to be sure the Fed is carrying out a monetary policy that will at least not stand in the way of his reelection and, if possible, underwrite it—quite literally. So the Fed is necessarily a political institution.

The Evolution of the Fed and Political Power

These four issues concerning central banks are inescapable. They are issues in American society and elsewhere. From the earliest days of our republic, the role of monetary policy, a "sound currency," was a central and controversial political issue. For example, after warrants had been issued to pay the troops during the American Revolution, the question was: "Are these debts that were incurred to fight for freedom and liberty of the Republic going to be paid off? Or are they going to be inflated away? Or are they going to be repudiated?" Those were the choices that faced the early republic.

Alexander Hamilton, the first secretary of the Treasury, is the one whose arguments prevailed on that occasion. He stated that if the new nation, the United States of America, was going to establish its creditworthiness in the world—that is, with the citizens and foreigners who had helped to underwrite the Revolution—there was no choice but to pay off the scrip. It must not repudiate its debts; it must, in fact, levy taxes on citizens to pay them off. In the debates that followed, Hamilton's position prevailed; the debts were assumed by the new government and were paid.

To deal with such problems, Congress subsequently passed two separate banking acts establishing the First and then the Second Bank of the United States, the charter of the first bank having lapsed in the interim. These were hardly central banks in the modern sense of the phrase. They were primarily development banks—funded by Congress to build canals, start industry, and, in effect, create an economy out of wilderness. But the arguments about their power and purpose were similar in a number of ways to the debates about the creation of the Fed.

From the beginning, these federally funded institutions had special privileges to which people not so privileged objected. The unprivileged made those objections more and more loudly understood over time. It was the populist president Andrew Jackson who, when he came to power in 1837, waged a battle against the monied interests and persuaded Congress to allow the charter of the Second Bank of the United States to lapse. He said, in effect, "This bank is an instrument of the monied classes. It does not belong as part of a society of democrats." As a result, there was no central bank, nor anything like it, for the rest of the nineteenth century. Those politics, together with issues of favoritism—paying off buddies, giving contracts to friends—which arise whenever there is the power to coin money, led to the demise of the early banks.

But the absence of a central monetary authority raised different kinds of problems. With the end of a federally chartered institution, wildcat banking flourished. ("Wildcat" banks were frontier institutions that printed their own banknotes, which served as cash in local regions but were of unreliable value.) Bank failures were commonplace. The need for some sort of regulation of wildcat banking, and the need to finance the Civil War, led to the National Banking Act of 1863. This institutional change was designed to bring order out of chaos, but it eventually brought about a political reaction as well. In the political campaign of 1896, William Jennings Bryan argued that the workers and farmers of America should not be "crucified upon a cross of gold." Sound money—its link to gold—was the primary issue of the campaign. In the 1890s the United States found itself in a major recession. Was sound money worth the price of unemployment and suffering?

These strands of history may seem of no great relevance to today's world. But the principles involved in these early battles are relevant to today's issues. Sound money versus prosperity is a theme that will not die. Out of similar historical fights came the establishment of the Federal Reserve System in 1914.

Big Politics and Little Politics

From its beginning, the Federal Reserve was caught up in both big and little politics. "Big politics" focused on issues of employment, the role of gold, the powers the Federal Reserve should have; "little politics" included jurisdictional battles among banks and banking districts. For example, it is not by happenstance that two of the regional banks are located in Missouri: one in St. Louis and one in Kansas City. That resulted from the fact that one of the senators from Missouri was a key member of the committee responsible for the Federal Reserve Act. He wanted to make sure that the Federal Reserve System, just like military contracts today, was an employment act and a power base for his constituency. Somewhere between big and little politics was the battle between Washington—the home of the Board of Governors of the Federal Reserve System—and the regional banks as a group. How was power to be distributed? This was also an issue between the Federal Reserve Bank of New York and the others. The power base of the Fed could not be located in New York, the center of financial interests. Politically, the only way to get the U.S. central bank accepted was to make it a *federal* system. The word "federal" in the Federal Reserve System has important political significance. The debate over who controls the power of the purse has echoed through history.[2]

Lack of experience also played an important part in the early design of the Federal Reserve System. We were an agricultural nation in 1914, far more so than today. An important question, therefore, was how one could have a monetary policy for the United States that took into account the differing economic conditions in Iowa, in the state of Washington, in Texas, and the like. Should not regional monetary policies reflect local conditions? Indeed, the twelve Fed districts were designed to implement regional monetary policies. Early on, however, it became clear that with a common currency, it was impossible to have differing regional monetary policies. The original idea that there could be different discount rates charged by the different regional Federal Reserve banks had to be scrapped. These same regional issues are slowing the march toward a European central bank today.

The Fed as a Quasi-Governmental Institution

Another important question in the development of the Fed has been that of the Fed's independence within the government. The Federal Reserve is a "quasi-governmental organization": it is chartered by Congress—there is no question that it is accountable, directly or indirectly, to the people through the Congress. The Constitution states that

Congress shall have the right to coin money and regulate the value thereof. Through legislation, the Congress has delegated that responsibility to the Fed.

The Federal Reserve is a creature of the Congress. But what does that mean? There is no doubt that the Congress can revise or repeal the Federal Reserve Act if it so chooses. It can and does, from time to time, modify the Federal Reserve Act. But Congress, naturally enough, likes to have it both ways. It wants someone to blame when the economy goes sour, and the Fed is a handy whipping boy. Congress is not likely to curb the power of the Fed in major ways. But it can threaten to change the Act when it thinks the Fed is overstepping, or when it wants the public to think that economic hardship is the result of a misspecified monetary policy.

It is useful to think of the Federal Reserve as independent *within* the government, not independent *of* the government. Before the 1930s, the linkage between administrations and the Federal Reserve was tighter than it has been subsequently. Specifically, by statute the secretary of the Treasury was a member of the Federal Reserve Board, and participated in discussions of monetary policy. The Comptroller of the Currency, who regulates national banks, was also a member of the Board of Governors until 1935.

That changed with the reforms of the 1930s. Those two officers—the secretary of the Treasury and the comptroller of the Currency—were, with their own approval, removed from the Fed's deliberations. With that change the Fed became more independent within the government.

A second political battle about the independence of the Federal Reserve occurred after World War II. Bill Martin, while he was assistant secretary of the Treasury, before becoming chairman of the Federal Reserve, negotiated an Accord between the Fed and the Treasury. The role of the Federal Reserve was very different during the wartime economy than it had been before or has been since. During the Second World War the key issue was how to get guns out of the production lines. Restricting credit was not an issue. Price and wage controls were used to control inflation. The role of the Fed was to support the issuance of government bonds to pay for the war and keep interest rates down.

As the Second World War ended, the United States struggled to get away from the controls that characterized the wartime economy. The

Treasury argued that the Fed should continue the practice of supporting the price of government bonds after the war. Bill Martin knew that
such a policy would tie the hands of the Fed in limiting inflation. As a
result of the Accord, it was the market, not the Fed, on which the
Treasury relied to sell its debt.

Another test of Fed independence occurred during the Vietnam
War. The Fed was appropriately worried about the inflationary pressures, and President Johnson was not prepared to ask Congress for an
unpopular tax increase to fight a very unpopular war. It was Bill Martin again who, as chairman, allowed an increase in Fed discount rates.
This enraged President Johnson, who saw the increase as an unpatri-
otic act on the part of the Fed.

To my knowledge, there have been no Federal Reserve chairmen
who have resigned because they had a major policy difference with an
administration. But that is the Fed's ultimate sanction. For example, if
a chairman of the Fed resigned and stated that the reason for resignation was disagreement with the profligate policies of a runaway spending government, that resignation would have major political
consequences. Chairmen do not have to use that stick to make their
power felt. And the Fed has power because it is by and large respected
in the Congress, even though it is chastised from time to time by
various members. The reputation that the Fed has established over a
period of decades stands it—and, I would argue, the country—in very
good stead.

That reputation was put to a test when Paul Volcker, whose essay
appears at the beginning of Part I of this volume, did the nation a great,
but controversial, service as Fed chairman in adopting a monetarist
approach—an adherence to a slower growth in monetary aggregates—
starting back in 1979, and staying with that monetarism for a period of
several years, precipitating a severe recession in the process, but purg-
ing the double-digit inflation of the late 1970s and early 1980s.

The Fed's conversion to monetarism was a marriage of conve-
nience, not of conviction. (Paul might describe it in different terms.)
The problem he faced was political. If the Fed were going to raise
interest rates to painfully high levels to clamp down on inflation, it
needed protection against its critics, especially those in Congress.
Monetarism provided the necessary rationale: high interest rates were
the result of market forces; the Fed was simply doing its job by controlling the growth of the money supply.

The political purpose in adopting monetarism was to raise a shield against criticism. But, once adopted, it was practiced as well as preached. It became the accepted theology of many central banks around the world: as Milton Friedman and others had argued, monetary policy, the theory said, should seek steady, stable, slow growth in the monetary aggregates (somehow defined) as *the* way to avoid the boom–bust cycles of credit expansion and contraction that had plagued the country. The Federal Reserve was not disingenuous; it really did guide policy during this period by establishing a range of growth for the money supply in the next six months, and adjusting interest rates if the actual figures were coming in outside the boundaries. Nineteen eighty-two was the peak year for interest rates. By 1983, the Fed began to abandon an exclusive focus on rates of growth in money.

One sometimes reads that the president or the chairman of the Council of Economic Advisers would like the Federal Reserve to ease monetary policy a little because the economy is still in recession. Such behind-the-scene tugging between an administration and the Federal Reserve is not unusual, and it raises the question of the Federal Reserve's role within the government. Should it make public statements about an administration's economic policy when it does not welcome advice from an administration about monetary policy? The administration officers who wield power on economic policy are the secretary of the Treasury, the chairman of the Council of Economic Advisers, and the director of the Office of Management and Budget (OMB). The chairman of the Federal Reserve is in an ambiguous position. When the first three get together over breakfast to talk about economic policy, does the chairman of the Fed get invited? Does he want to be invited? In candor, he would probably like to be present, but not held responsible!

The presidency is a powerful office. I find it hard to imagine circumstances in which the president would ask Congress to force the Fed to change policy. There are far more subtle and effective ways of delivering the message. One is simply to have the chairman of the Council of Economic Advisers talk to the press either on background or for attribution about the state of the economy: "It's not responding, the banks are not lending money, we've got to get the Federal Reserve to reduce interest rates and make credit more available—or the Fed will be responsible." Put the Fed publicly on notice that it will be held responsible for the suffering of the American people. That is a pretty effective sanction. It does not take crude power plays; it comes down to "open-mouth policy."

Secrecy at the Fed is another issue that is sometimes a focus for political debate. For years there was a one-year delay in the publication of the minutes of the Open Market Committee's meetings. You can imagine how that played in Hometown, America. It really did not go over very well. Thus, it is only natural that the issue arose of how soon and how fully the minutes of these meetings would be published and even whether meetings would be secret in the first place. The current compromise is that the Fed now publishes the minutes of its meetings with a one-month delay.

Another aspect of political control concerns supervisory power over Fed spending. The Federal Reserve spends a lot of money each year running the payments system and supervising the banking system. Whose money is it? Is this taxpayers' money that is being spent by the independent Federal Reserve? Or is it somehow manna from heaven that descends upon the Fed? (That is metaphorical, I hope you understand.) The issue is an important one. Who controls the purse of the Fed? Technically, the Fed buys government securities as a primary way of putting reserves into the banking system. It earns interest on those government securities. That interest more than pays for the costs of running the Federal Reserve System. Each year the Fed pays back to the Treasury the excess of what it earns on government securities over its costs. But who is going to say whether it is running the System effectively or not?

The watchdog of Congress is the General Accounting Office (GAO). The GAO oversees every government agency on behalf of Congress. But the Fed is only a quasi-public institution. It did not believe that the General Accounting Office should have the right to walk in the door of Federal Reserve banks and the Federal Reserve Board of Governors and look at the books. The Fed saw it as interference with its independence. After some tense negotiations, the General Accounting Office prevailed in its right to look over the shoulder of the Federal Reserve System with respect to its expenditures. The General Accounting Office does *not* have the authority to review the policy decisions with respect to monetary policy. So the spending of taxpayers' dollars has accountability, but the policy decisions of the independent Federal Reserve are still independent.

Another area of some controversy between the Fed and Congress concerns the appointment of the presidents of the Federal Reserve banks. The issue is whether bank presidents, who vote on monetary policy, should be appointed by the president and confirmed by the Senate, as is the case with Fed governors. Currently they are selected by their boards of directors with the concurrence of the Board of Governors.

Finally, with respect to Congress's oversight of the Fed, the Chairman now reports every six months to the Banking Committees, explaining the Fed's stewardship and looking ahead to the next year's economy, and what the Fed is going to do about it. This requirement began with the passage of the Humphrey–Hawkins Act and is now built into the institutional structure.

Pressures on the Fed can occasionally become extraordinary. In the 1970s, when Arthur Burns was up for reappointment as chairman, a member of the White House staff leaked groundless stories to the press about Arthur Burns's personal spending. These were scurrilous efforts to discredit the personal behavior of a man who was above reproach.

In a similar vein, Dewey Daane recounts the following incident. In December 1965, during the Vietnam War, it became clear that Dewey's was the deciding vote needed by the administration to preserve an accommodative monetary policy. Martin and two others were clearly for a discount rate increase; three of the liberal Democrats were against it. The White House approached Secretary of the Treasury Fowler, a close personal friend of Dewey's, who invited Dewey down to Florida, and in his customary, courteous way—he was very much the southern gentleman—he laid out the case against the discount rate increase. Dewey finished his breakfast, and then he said to Mr. Fowler, "Mr. Secretary, I appreciate your courtesy and I will certainly give it every consideration. I'm not convinced by your case."

Dewey flew back to Washington and was met by a Fed driver to take him to the Board—this meeting on the discount rate was contingent on his return. The driver said, "The undersecretary of the Treasury needs to see you before you go into the meeting." When Dewey stopped at the Treasury, he was told, flat out, that if he voted for the increase, he would never have another job in Washington or any other place; both Fowler and the president would see to it. Dewey nevertheless voted for the increase in the discount rate. Two months later, the president and the secretary of the Treasury were publicly acknowledging it was the right move.

Central banks were not created to be loved, but to be respected. They have an important set of tasks to perform—supervising the payments mechanism and ensuring the value of the currency. They have important powers and responsibilities.

In the United States, the Federal Reserve is ultimately accountable to the Congress. How that accountability is discharged—and how the relationship between the Fed and an administration is determined—are subjects of continuing political debate. Most people believe that money will not manage itself. If that is true, then a central bank is an uncomfortable necessity. And history seems to indicate that to do its job effectively, a central bank needs a distancing from day-to-day politics—whether leaders be kings, presidents, or congressmen. Independence within the government is a democratic compromise that pragmatically reconciles independence and accountability.

Notes

1. More specifically, they can ruin an economy if they are not well organized; they do not have the power to make things right if everything else is going wrong.

2. The issues remain important today. In talking with a group of Russian parliamentarians who were in Washington in July 1991 before the attempted coup, I found it was one of the things in which they were most interested. They wanted to understand the linkages between central government, republics (here, states), and local governments in our system, as they tried to rearrange and construct the whole issue of federalism in the former Soviet Union.

7

David M. Jones

Monetary Policy as Viewed by a Money Market Participant

Economic policymaking is an art, not a science. It is an art because of the nature of the empirical evidence one has to work with. In a natural science, theorizing can be separated from testing. Scientific tests can be carried out in a controlled environment, precisely measuring the effect of one variable on another, holding other things equal. In economic policy, it cannot. In economic policymaking, forecasting is imperfect. Good judgment and an instinct for good timing are at least as important to economic policymakers as prowess in theoretical model building, technical knowledge, or number-crunching abilities.

This is not to say that one's understanding of the economy, which determines one's forecasts, is not tested. For example, the theories underlying my forecasts are tested daily in the trading room. All too often some poor Treasury bill trader says, "Jones! You told me interest rates were going down last week! They went *up*! What are you going to say about that?" I say, "Wait a minute! I've got this big theory in economics! In six months I'm sure I'll be right!" The trader says, "Jones! How much money will I lose before you're right?"

It is such interaction of theory and real-world conditions that leads any forecaster away from science and into art. In the trading room, where the real world exists, they are taking into account psychology, technical supply conditions, domestic financial and economic conditions, global conditions, and all the rest. Unquestionably, you want to take all that into account too. And all economic forecasters I know do so.

In order to discuss the art of forecasting, you must first have a good sense of the mechanisms of Fed policy—the process, tools, targets, goals, and definitions. The Greenspan Fed's ultimate targets are stable prices and sustainable growth. The Greenspan Fed favors a myriad of intermediate indicators to be used in determining when Fed policy shifts are appropriate. Among these intermediate indicators are money and credit growth, and important coincident signals of real growth such as nonfarm payroll employment. Other intermediate indicators that signal inflation would include commodity prices. Figure 7.1 shows the intermediate indicators used by the Fed.

My starting point for an interest rate forecast is the Federal Reserve. The Fed has its primary influence on short-term rates. To determine short-term rates we must take into account Federal Reserve policy shifts and business loan demand, among other factors. In forecasting long-term interest rates, other factors, such as inflationary expectations, and the financial burden and uncertainty associated with the federal budget deficit, must also be taken into account. Short-term rates are related to long-term rates in the "yield curve." Table 7.1 shows the Fed's policy shifts for 1991, a year when there was a substantial lowering of the Fed funds rate. The relationship between short-term and long-term rates can be seen in Figure 7.2b. Also, note the relationship between U.S. and foreign long-term interest rates in Figure 7.2d.

In Figure 7.1, please note that the seven Fed governors and the five voting Reserve Bank presidents make up the most important Fed policymaking body—the Federal Open Market Committee (FOMC). The FOMC's primary policy guidelines are, at present, the federal funds rate and depository institutions' borrowings at the Fed discount window. The federal funds rate is the rate on bank reserve balances at the Fed that are loaned and borrowed among banks, usually overnight.

In attempting to anticipate Fed policy shifts, I use information about each Fed governor and district president who is on the FOMC. Let me give an example. Alan Greenspan is a first-class numbers cruncher. Some say that there has never been a number he did not like. But there are some intermediate indicators listed in Figure 7.1 that Greenspan likes more than others. The monthly nonfarm payroll employment figure is one of them. Essentially, this number comes from a monthly Bureau of Labor Statistics (BLS) survey of about 360,000 businesses. These business establishments tell BLS survey teams how many people have been added to their payrolls and how many have been subtracted from their payrolls.

The nonfarm payroll employment figure is separate from the data

Figure 7.1 Fed Policy Objectives, Intermediate Indicators, and Alternative Open Market Operating Procedures

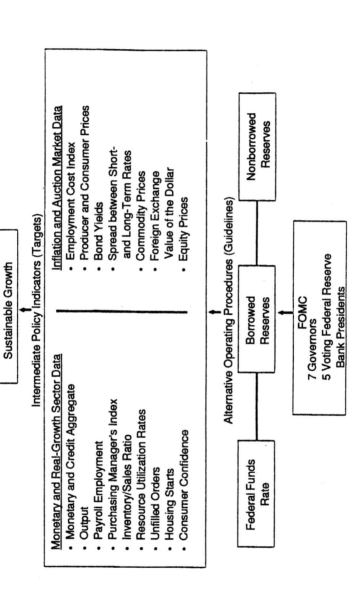

Figure 7.2 Interrelated Interest Rates

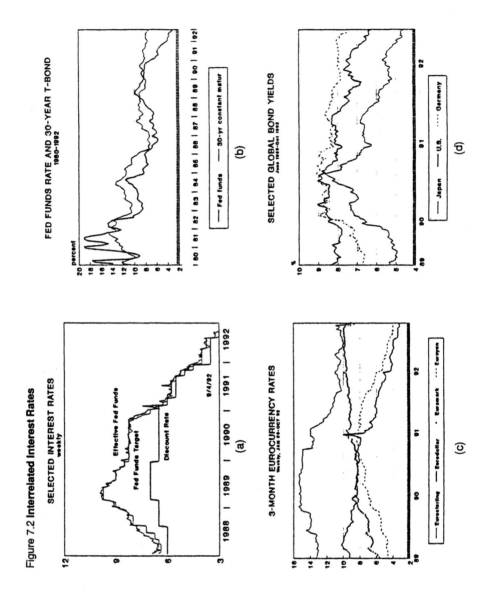

Table 7.1

Actual and Estimated Fed Policy Shifts In 1991

	Type of Fed Shift in Reserve Pressures	Fed Borrowings Target (millions $)	Associated Fed Funds Rate (percent)	Discount Rate (percent)
January 9	Modest easing	100	6.75	
February 1	Full "pass through"	100	6.25	6(2/1/91)
March 8	Modest easing	75	6.00	
March 21	No change	125	6.00	
April 18	No change	150	6.00	
April 30	Partial "pass through"	175	5.75	5.50 (4/30/91)
May 2	No change	200	5.75	
May 16	No change	225	5.75	
June 13	No change	250	5.75	
June 20	No change	275	5.75	
June 27	No change	325	5.75	
July 11	No change	350	5.75	
July 25	No change	400	5.75	
August 6	Modest easing	375	5.50	
September 5	No change	350	5.50	
September 12	No change	300	5.50	
September 13	Partial "pass through"	325	5.25	5 (9/13/91)
October 3	No change	300	5.25	
October 10	No change	275	5.25	
October 17	No change	250	5.25	
October 31	Modest easing	175	5.00	
November 6	Partial "pass through"	175	4.75	4.50 (11/6/91)
November 7	No change	150	4.75	
November 14	No change	125	4.75	
November 29	No change	100	4.75	
December 6	Modest easing	75	4.50	
December 20	Partial "pass through"	100	4.00	3.50 (12/20/91)

used to calculate the unemployment rate, which comes out at the same time. The unemployment rate is based on a BLS household survey—asking households whether their members have been looking for jobs during the past four weeks and have not found any. The household unemployment figures also come out each month.

The nonfarm payroll employment survey covers the goods-producing and services sectors. There are about 110 million people on nonfarm payrolls at present. About 25 percent of that payroll employment is goods-producing and about 75 percent of that total is service industries.

Greenspan, in eight out of the Fed's eighteen easing moves between July 1990 and September 1992, has changed policy largely on the basis of the nonfarm payroll employment monthly number. Bang! The number comes out on the first Friday of a given month; it is a lot weaker than people think. In the early stages of a normal recovery, nonfarm payrolls should be increasing by 300,000 to 400,000 workers per month. If that number falls, as it has at times during the current recovery, Greenspan will promptly swing into action and lower rates. For example, on December 7, 1990, and again on February 1, March 8, and December 6, 1991, as well as on July 2 and September 4, 1992, the nonfarm payroll figure turned out weaker than he and others expected, and so Greenspan changed policy on the same day as the release of the weaker-than-expected payroll figure. Also, on January 8 and August 6, 1991, the Fed eased within two business days of the release of unexpected weak payroll figures. If I am predicting interest rates, that information is important.

Another data set Greenspan likes is the corporate purchasing managers' index. Basically, you have about 360 purchasing managers buying supplies and materials for companies that, on the first of every month, report on orders, production, employment, and price pressures. In my view, this index focuses too much on the industrial sector. It misses important movements in the service sector. Nevertheless, Greenspan is a recognized master of industrial-sector analysis; he is highly effective in identifying real-sector imbalances, as reflected in inventory adjustments.

To give you an example of how much of a numbers cruncher Greenspan is, let me recount a story. I walked into his office right after he moved in. He had the office redecorated at the Federal Reserve Board in Washington. Paul Volcker had darkened the white walls with cigar smoke. Moreover, Volcker had a door that opened onto the hallway, making it possible for people walking down the hall to eavesdrop on the chairman's conversations inside. Greenspan closed off the door opening onto the hallway and installed a new bookcase covering the space, secretizing the chairman's office. The office was also newly painted. Greenspan had his shirtsleeves rolled up, and he walked up and said, "David . . ." and I expected him to say, "How do you do?"

and, "How have you been?" Instead, he said, "Do you have any data on inventories of imported goods?" Those were the first words out of his mouth. Now, that's a guy who loves numbers.

Why is this important? Because his vision of the economy will be shaped by those numbers that he favors. By way of contrast, Greenspan, in most instances, places less emphasis on anecdotal information or simple policy instinct. And if you are predicting interest rates, you want to know how the chairman of the Federal Reserve Board sees the economic situation in quantitative terms which will bear on how he decides to shift policy.

David Mullins, the vice chairman of the Fed Board of Governors, is a rising star at the Fed and an increasingly influential policymaker. Mullins favors market indicators such as the shape of the yield curve. For example, if the yield curve steepens sharply in response to Fed easing actions (as the Fed pushes short-term rates down relative to long-term rates) this would be taken by Mullins as a signal that bond market investors view the Fed's easing actions as excessive and potentially inflationary. Most alarming to Mullins and other Fed policymakers focusing on market indicators would be a situation in which a Fed move to push short-term rates lower is viewed as easing excessively and long-term rates actually increase.

The Fed's use of the yield curve (or the spread between short- and long-term interest rates) as an intermediate policy indicator is grounded in neo-Wicksellian theory. The best approximation of Wicksell's "bank rate" is the federal funds rate, and of his "natural rate," the long-term Treasury bond rate. According to Wicksellian theory, the "natural rate" is the hypothetical cost of capital that would balance savings and investment in the economy at stable prices. Wicksellian theory holds that so long as the bank rate is close to the natural rate, the rate of increase in prices will be stable or declining.

If you are forecasting interest rates, you would also want to know all about the FOMC and its participants. It formally meets about eight times a year. Besides these formal meetings, the members meet in special telephone conference meetings in between regularly scheduled meetings if something unexpected comes up about the economy or the financial system.[1]

Most importantly, you should also examine closely the interaction between the most influential Fed policymakers. In particular, you should watch closely the interaction between the politically independent Fed chairman (whose selection is greatly influenced by financial market opinion) and the more politically attuned vice chairman of the Board of Governors (who, in modern times, has been carefully chosen by the administration in power for assertiveness within Fed policy circles and sensitivity to administration concerns). Financial market participants demand, as a condition for their support, that prospective Fed chairmen swear that they will be independent of partisan political pressures. The current Fed chairman, Alan Greenspan, was clearly the favorite of the financial markets. And his predecessor, Paul Volcker, might neither have been appointed initially by the Carter administration nor reappointed by the Reagan administration were it not for his extremely high standing in financial market opinion. In contrast, the three most recent vice chairmen of the Federal Reserve Board were politically involved with the executive branch when chosen. They were all widely quoted in the press and highly visible in a job that previously had virtually no visibility. They include Preston Martin and Manuel Johnson, both of whom had close ties to the Reagan administration when chosen as Fed Board vice chairmen, and David Mullins, the current vice chairman of the Fed Board, who was close to the Bush administration. Another influential policymaking position is that of vice chairman of the FOMC, which is occupied by the president of the Federal Reserve Bank of New York. The New York Reserve Bank president is the only Reserve Bank president who has a permanent vote on the FOMC.

In predicting the economy, another thing that plays a role is a feel for the economy. In 1990, for example, the numbers were good but there was a feel of eroding confidence in the air. It was a "confidence" recession and one influenced by a "credit crunch." If you look at loan figures for banks, you see they fell substantially. Business loans, mortgage loans—any kind of loans. It was the biggest crash in lending activity I have ever seen. Now, it is true that in a recession, loan demand usually falls. Good businesses are not going to take risks in a recession and so they concentrate on restructuring debt and their loan demand slumps. So part of this contracting loan activity could reflect weak loan demand, but part of it also has to do, to an important degree, with sudden and arbitrary limits on the *supply* of depository institution credit to businesses and individuals, especially in 1990 and 1991. I have never seen, in my entire experience, as much restraint on the loan supply side as we had in 1990–91. In those years, we had a greater contraction in total loans by all these depository institutions than at any time since the depths of the Great Depression. For many borrowers, alternative sources of credit in the capital markets are simply not available. When you look at that loan data, you will understand why I was so concerned about what was ahead for our economy in that time period.

What is the appropriate model for that experience? What decade? The 1930s. The current models were of little use in analyzing the 1990–91 experience because they were based on real-sector imbalances and inventory adjustments during an average postwar inventory recession. But the slow-growth experience of the early 1990s largely reflected financial strains rather than real-sector imbalances. Inventory recessions could be seen in adjustments in business inventories. In the early 1990s we had a financial or balance sheet recession. It was essentially a conflict between an overleveraged economy clashing with banks that were unusually reluctant to make new loans. This was the most dangerous recession we had been in since the 1930s because the models to help us understand how to get us out of it simply did not work. Inventory imbalances were not the primary problem. Instead, it was a balance sheet problem. We needed to give individuals and businesses time to restructure debt in a declining interest rate environment and let banks work through their bad loans and improve their financial strength before they were willing to make any new loans.

A while back, I met with the top forty homebuilders in the country. There also happened to be one banker at the meeting. The homebuilders said, "We're being cut off totally from new loans by this crunch." And the banker said, "Look, folks. I'll lend you money when I work out of my bad loans made in the roaring 1980s. I can do better getting a loan reclassified from 'bad,' on which I have to hold loan loss reserves and take a hit on profits, to 'good,' than I can making a new, possibly risky loan, even on a net interest spread of almost 300 basis points, or 3 percentage points. And I'm not lending you any money till I get rid of the bad loans, get them reclassified to good loans, work through them with the borrowers." And the builders said, "When might that be?" And the banker said, "In about three years [1994]." Meanwhile, banks were benefiting from an unusually wide net interest margin, and increasing their liquidity in the form of heavy purchases of safe U.S. government securities. At the same time, banks gradually improved their capital positions. That is the real-world part of this policy picture.

My view of the 1991 recession was that it was not a typical V-shaped recession. The typical contraction is based on inventory overhangs and cutbacks in orders, production, and employment. Then, immediately after the bottom of the recession is reached, the economy bounces back up.

I believed that the experience was more dangerous than that. It was a balance sheet recession started by a credit crunch that severely limited the *supply* of credit in 1990–91. This credit crunch triggered a prolonged period of recession and weak economic growth accompanied by a decline in the *demand* for credit in 1992–93. This cut-off in the supply of bank credit was aggravated by weakened consumer and business balance sheets reflecting, on the liability side, the excessive debt buildup of the 1980s and, on the asset side, sharply declining prices of real estate and other real assets previously inflated in the 1980s. I predicted that the shape of the balance sheet recession and recovery would be more like a small "w." I even argued that we could have another falloff; it could be a triple-dip recession. It could be spread out like a small "w" with an extra loop. I further predicted that it might be 1994 before this economy starts to recover on a sustained basis.[2]

Where does the Fed fit into all this? The Fed is like a doctor diagnosing a patient, the economy. It is continually looking for indicators of trouble in the economy—using, in the Greenspan Fed's case, the intermediate policy indicators shown in Figure 7.1—to determine when to shift policy. The operating room is the FOMC. There are twelve surgeons conducting the operations.

Now, try to put yourself in the place of the twelve people who have to make policy. Twelve economists, twenty-four different answers. They all differ with each other, and then change their minds at least once during the debate. So how do you get an answer? It is not easy. In essence, Fed policymakers respond partly to unforeseen economic developments and partly to anticipated economic trends. In any event, the Fed eased its key policy lever—the Fed funds rate—two dozen times between June 1989 and September 1992. The economic response, in contrast with past recoveries, has been weak and uneven and insufficient to tame a high and unruly unemployment rate. All that the Fed has been able to do so far is make it easier for debt restructuring and to improve the health of the banking system, which should help build the foundation for future expansion. We are in a prolonged period of financial strain that might be called a "contained financial contraction."

There is inevitably an argument within the Fed about how tough the Fed should be on inflation. During the 1979–84 period in particular, the Volcker Fed had the single-minded purpose of defeating inflation and inflation psychology. More recently, the Greenspan Fed has been trying to juggle the two ultimate objectives of stable prices and sustainable growth.

Fed Operating Features

The Fed operating procedures are straightforward. Until 1979 the Fed had a very simple system. It focused exclusively on the Fed funds rate as its operating guideline. The Fed funds rate is the key short-term interest rate for all the financial markets. It is the rate most responsive to Fed policy changes; it is the rate that the Fed directly influences when it changes policy; and, under the Greenspan Fed, changes in the Federal funds rate are still the best signal to use in determining when he is changing policy. From 1979 to 1982 the Fed targeted the supply of nonborrowed reserves. From 1982 to 1987, the Fed focused primarily on a borrowings guideline.

Since 1987, the Greenspan Fed has focused on twin operating guidelines: borrowings and the Fed funds rate. By borrowings, I mean bank borrowings at the Federal Reserve discount window (the middle square in the lower panel of Figure 7.1). Under Alan Greenspan, when the Fed wants to tighten policy, typically what will happen is that there will be a quarter-percent change in the funds rate—let's say from 5.25 percent to 5.5 percent—associated with roughly a $50–$100 million increase in the Fed borrowings target. Conversely, if the Fed is easing policy, say from 5.25 percent to 5 percent, there would be a related *decline* of $50–$100 million in the Fed borrowings target. I should note that, more recently, bank aversion to borrowing reserves at the Fed discount window has increased, owing to the fact that increased bank discount window borrowings are viewed as a sign of bank weakness in the current period of financial system stress. Thus, the present relationship involves a much smaller $25 million increase in discount window borrowings for each one-quarter percentage point increase in the Fed funds rate and, conversely, a $25 million decline in borrowings is associated with each one quarter-percentage point decline in the Fed funds rate.

Currently, this borrowings target level is only about $200–$300 million, and total reserves in the banking system are about $50 billion. So borrowed reserves are a very small piece of total reserves, leaving $49.7 or $49.8 billion of nonborrowed reserves. Even though borrowings are an infinitesimal part of the reserves total, they are the most sensitive indicator of Fed-induced changes in reserve pressures. The Fed has joint operating guidelines of the Fed funds rate and borrowed reserves. To predict interest rates, one must watch how the Fed intervenes in the market in order to influence this Fed funds rate. After some early miscommunication with the financial markets over signals of Fed policy shifts (notably in the case of the so-called Thanksgiving Fiasco of November 1989), the Greenspan Fed has more recently sought (with considerable success) to communicate its policy intentions more clearly. For example, Fed System one-day repurchase agreements (RPs) at the prevailing Fed funds rate level suggest that the Fed's intention is to ease its stance. Or, if market-easing psychology has already pushed the Fed funds down to the Fed's newly desired lower funds rate level, the Fed would do a less aggressive customer RP to signal its easing intentions. (Fed System RPs represent Fed actions to inject reserves temporarily into the banking system through repurchase agreements to buy U.S. government securities; Fed customer RPs are transactions in which the Fed acts as an agent for customers by investing the customers' funds temporarily in money market RP's, thereby reducing the drain on bank reserves that would otherwise have occurred if these customer funds had instead been invested internally at the Fed in the form of a reverse RP.)

Notice that I have said nothing about textbook reserve–money multipliers? Now, it is true that we *do* have a reserve multiplier, and that for every dollar of reserves the Fed injects into the system there is a multiple of several dollars in terms of potential credit and deposit expansion in the banking system. But when you are analyzing Fed policy, and analyzing the levers of policy, you watch some simple breakdowns that the Fed watches. In my world, the textbook multiplier relationship is almost irrelevant. The primary rule of Fed watching is to "watch" the same breakdown of the reserve total into borrowed and nonborrowed reserves that the Fed "watches." In measuring shifts in pressures on bank reserve positions, the Fed actually "watches" the borrowed reserve component of total reserves more closely than the reserve base or total reserves.

Remember, when you watch the Fed, you watch what it actually watches, not what you think it *should* watch. And what the Fed is watching as operating guidelines is three things: the Fed funds rate, borrowed reserves, and, at least during the 1979–82 period, non-borrowed reserves. They *don't use* fancy textbook theory or hypothetical reserve multiplier relationships.

When you want to analyze real-world monetary policy, you must get into the context of the Fed decision, and that means focusing on the two levers on the left-hand side of the lower panel of Figure 7.1 with the heading "operating procedures" (or guidelines): the funds rate and the borrowed reserves level. The FOMC does nothing more complicated than to say, "If we want to tighten, we squeeze banks by cutting back on nonborrowed reserve growth; we tighten pressures on bank reserve positions and force them into the discount window temporarily to borrow an extra $50–$100 million in funds." Then individual banks must soon get out of the discount window because of surveillance and the tradition against borrowing. These banks are going to scramble around and bid up the Fed funds rate as they try to increase their footings of loanable funds in order to support new loan activity. Thus, we have a positive association between higher borrowings and a higher Fed funds rate. Conversely, when the Fed is easing its policy stance, there is a relationship between a decline in discount window borrowings and a drop in the Fed funds rate.

If one were looking at theoretical conventions, the effect of such policy shifts on the economy might be considered minimal. But the policy works as a signal. With it the Fed tells the market: "We've slowed down reserve growth; we've more than offset the effect of market factors on bank reserve positions; we've curtailed the availability of reserves to the whole banking system and forced banks into the window to borrow an extra $50–$100 million temporarily." Then banks are forced eventually to step up their bidding for alternative sources of short-term loanable funds, thus leading to an increase (usually one-quarter percentage point) in the Fed funds rate. Of course, the Fed may also take larger and more dramatic tightening (or easing) steps, but, for the most part, the Greenspan Fed has been content to change policy in small (but often frequent) steps that could easily be reversed if necessary.

The monetary authorities can also influence the Fed funds rate though adjustments in the discount rate, which is the rate that the

Federal Reserve charges depository institutions for the privilege of borrowing at the discount window. For example, on September 13, 1991, the discount rate was lowered from 5.25 percent to 5 percent. The Fed allowed only a quarter-point pass through in the funds rate to 5.25 percent from 5.5 percent; they did that through a manipulation of the borrowings target, actually tightening it a little bit to prevent a full half-point pass through in the Fed funds rate, associated with the half-point decline in the discount rate.

To understand how borrowings fit into the picture, you must recognize that there is a bank tradition against borrowing. In 1984, Continental Bank faced a liquidity crisis and got into real trouble. As a financial institution in difficulty, Continental Bank borrowed $6 or $7 billion from the discount window. And what was that? It was a symptom of a bank in trouble. Market observers concluded that if you run your bank so badly that you have got to go into the discount window for $6 or $7 billion, you must not be very good. Also operating to make borrowed reserves at the discount window different from other sources of reserves is Fed surveillance of the purpose, frequency, and size of depository institution borrowings at the discount window.

Thus, as a rule, borrowings, not total reserves, are the most sensitive indicators of changes in Fed policy. When borrowings go up as a share of the reserve total, you get this tightening pressure gauge effect: borrowings go up, bank reserve pressures tighten, the bank eventually has to fall back on the funds market or other sources of funds, and the Fed funds rate goes up. Conversely, when the Fed relieves the pressure on bank reserve positions, borrowings will go down, and the funds rate will go down.

A final note to remember is that in following movements of these variables, it is fundamentally important to separate offensive Fed actions from defensive Fed actions. Defensive Fed actions come in response to movements caused by other market factors affecting bank reserve availability. One of those other factors is float, which affects reserves independently of the Fed. Float is created when checks in the process of collection are not collected on time. The Federal Reserve gives banks extra credit for checks that are not collected according to a set time schedule, and this increases total reserves. When the Fed acts through open market operations to drain reserves in order to offset the increase in reserves from a rise in float, this is not a signal of a policy change. This is a defensive action. Other market factors influencing bank reserves independently of the Fed include Treasury deposits at the Fed and currency in circulation.

The basics are easy; but to interpret any particular Fed easing steps you must also know all the components of discount window borrowings. For example, *seasonal* borrowings are borrowings by small banks in farm communities and tourist areas that can get advances at the discount window for several weeks at a time to offset heavy increases in loan demand for crop planting or to counter the negative reserve impact of tourists' demands for currency in circulation. Within each year, seasonal borrowings rise from a low in January to a peak in August. The other types of borrowing at the Fed discount window include temporary *adjustment* borrowings, to meet unforeseen increases in loan demand or deposit outflows, and *extended credit* borrowing by financial institutions in difficulty. The best gauge of Fed-induced changes in pressure on bank reserve positions for policy purposes is *adjustment* plus *seasonal* borrowings at the discount window.

The Effect of Monetary Policy on the Economy

What does all the above Fed institutional and operational detail have to do with the economy? In essence, the Fed funds rate represents the primary cost of short-term loanable funds and will influence the prime bank lending rate. The Fed's primary impact is usually on short-term rates, but at times longer-term rates will follow suit. These are costs to borrowers. Changing these interest rates will then affect aggregate demand: consumer buying of cars, and purchases of other big-ticket items. Changes in interest rates also affect home buying and business capital spending.

So a Fed tightening action has affected the cost and to some degree the availability of money and credit. If it costs you more to borrow, and you are having trouble finding the money, then aggregate demand—particularly by consumers for big-ticket items like cars, furniture, and appliances—and business capital spending will be depressed by higher interest rates; this in turn will dampen aggregate real output growth, or real GDP, and then eventually inflation. So the whole story unfolds. Underlying this story is a modified Keynesian aggregate demand model in which real output responds to shifts in demand. You are working toward affecting aggregate demand, which in turn will affect how fast output grows, as measured by real GDP, which in turn affects price pressures.

Not everyone accepts this story. The monetarists on the Fed Board say it is all wrong. Just hit a monetary target. Other Fed Governors worry about commodity prices and other market signals—including futures and option market signals. This is an important point: there seem to be nearly as many theories of how policy interacts with the economy as there are members of the FOMC. But ultimately even the most complicated theories must be applied to the real world. In the end, Fed officials must agree on actual policy decisions to deal with the actual economic world.

Why Is Monetary Policy So Important?

Why is understanding monetary policy so important? Because monetary policy is the only game in town. Monetary policy is, by default, the government's most effective and flexible policy tool. Politics, not economics, determines fiscal policy. Thus, it cannot be expected that fiscal policy (changes in federal taxes and spending) will influence the economy in a timely manner. Today, the pursuit of the policy goal of sustainable, noninflationary growth falls on the Fed's shoulders. Under present circumstances, if the economy is to be controlled effectively, it will be through monetary policy.

Notes

1. Nancy Teeters, who was one of the prominent governors and a respected model for the modern professional career woman with a family, and who went on to become chief economist for IBM, tells a story of one of these conference calls. She was down in North Carolina on vacation with her kids running riot. She was stirring a pot of stew on the stove and had the telephone in one hand, deciding on monetary policy. She would stir that pot of stew and say, "No, no—we should ease reserve pressures in order to speed up the growth of M_2."

2. Editors' note: These predictions were made in September 1991, and they have largely come true.

8

Eugene A. Leonard

A Monetarist's Confession

I confess: I have not always known the truth. I am a monetarist by conversion, not birth. I was trained at Missouri as a neo-Keynesian. What changed me and taught me the truth was seventeen years at the Federal Reserve Bank of St. Louis. Converts such as I do, however, have a sense of sin and a sense of truth that birthright monetarists do not have, and in this essay I will try to give you a sense of the monetarist truth.

The thing that converted me was the evidence. Theory is one thing, but evidence is another. I became aware, for example, that in the 1960s and 1970s a rising trend in the rate of inflation was accompanied by higher rather than lower unemployment rates. Further, I saw that progressively more stimulative monetary policy over this same twenty-year period (that is, higher and higher rates of money growth) did nothing, on balance, to stimulate real economic output. Only nominal gross national product, which includes inflation, grew at a progressively more rapid rate.

Finally, and perhaps most revealing of all, was the fact that there seemed to be a strong relationship between sharp and sustained changes in money growth and business cycle behavior, to wit: each of the four recessions between 1960 and 1980 was preceded by, or coincided with, a time period of two calendar quarters or more in which the rate of money growth fell below its long-term trend. This convinced me that changes in money growth had a destabilizing influence on the economy—a rather disturbing feeling since I was working for the central bank, which was chartered in significant measure to promote stability! I came to be a believer in monetarism.

What Is Monetarism?

So, what is this thing we call monetarism, and what do monetarists believe?

First of all, monetarists believe that money influences the economy in two very separate and very distinct ways. The first one has to do with the long run, and the second has to do with shorter periods of time relevant to the business cycle—periods of several months up to a few years.

The Role of Money in the Long Run

In the long run, almost all economists believe that the trend of money growth is going to determine the trend in the price level. When we say "the long run," we are talking about a period of several or many years. In countries where you have rapid rates of money growth, you are going to have rapid rates of inflation. In countries where you have slow rates of money growth, you will have slow rates of inflation. In fact, in the United States between the Civil War and the turn of the century, we actually had declining prices, even though it was a period of very rapid economic growth. This was the heyday of the Industrial Revolution, of capitalism, of enormous rates of increase in real wealth and production and productivity. Why did we have declining prices during this period? Because we had a declining money supply.

This long-run relationship is one of the important tenets of monetarism: that over time the rate of money growth does determine the price level. The rate of money growth does not determine the rate of real output. Real output depends on real things: factors of production, land, labor, capital, and the human factor. So real output, in the long run, is going to be determined by real resources, including human resources, and not by the rate of money growth.[1] In the monetarist creed, money determines prices; money does not determine real output.

The implication of the monetarist creed is that if money does not determine real output in the long run, governments and central banks are foolish to attempt to coax more product out of the economy by increasing the money supply. The evidence, to which I referred earlier, was this: in 1960, we had a trend (five-year moving average) of growth in the M_1 supply of less than 2 percent. By 1980, this trend had accelerated to well over 7 percent. Yet there was absolutely no improvement in real economic growth to compensate for the increase in money growth and the accompanying higher rate of inflation.

The Role of Money in the Short Run

Monetarists believe that the economy is inherently stable. And since the economy tends toward stability, if left to its own devices it will be more or less stable over time. Empirical evidence does not answer the question of how stable the economy is one way or the other, so it is a point of faith, just as it is a point of faith for Keynesians that the economy is unstable. This means, for monetarists, that the short run refers to cycles around a stable trend. These cycles last between several months and a few years.

What are the kinds of interferences that stand in the way of stability in the economy? Some of them are quite beyond the control of the central bank, or of the government, for that matter. I am talking now about things like plagues or disease or pests or famine; about drought, earthquakes, hurricanes, natural disasters; I am talking about geopolitical events like the Berlin Wall coming down or the collapse of communism inside the Soviet Union; about war in the Persian Gulf, or, going back to the 1970s, the OPEC action that quadrupled the price of oil overnight in the fall of 1973. All of these things are shocks to the economy.

All of these events are going to cause something else to happen. Output is going to change as a result. The monetarist acknowledges that all these things are beyond the control of our government, and they are going to impact on real output, and there really is not a whole hell of a lot that we can do about it.

But we do feel that once these shocks have had their impact on the economy, the economy will then tend to recover and move back toward stability rather than being thrown out of kilter and being sent off in some kind of wild direction permanently.

Monetarists also believe that there are not very many times when the types of events that I have just described are going to happen in such combination and in such coincidence to really cause a serious enough impact on output to create recession. They will cause minor disturbances in output, but they will not conspire very often to really slow the economy into recession in and of themselves.

What I am building up to—and you have probably heard Milton Friedman quoted on this subject—is that monetarists believe that in most instances, the phenomena that are described and labeled and defined as recessions are not caused so much by natural events that are beyond our control, but, rather, by monetary events. And so the second thing that monetarists believe is really important is that over the shorter period of time—the ups and downs of the business cycle—sharp fluctuations in money growth, sharp changes in money growth from whatever the underlying trend happens to be at the time, can have an impact on output and employment and thus on interest rates.

The mechanism by which a sharp and sustained change in money growth will affect the economy is poorly understood. Sometimes it is referred to as "the black box": you pour money into this black box, and somehow it has an influence on the economy. But real-world economists have little problem with black boxes. We are interested in what goes in and what comes out, not what is inside.

The black box is not a magic box; there is a common-sense explanation of the relationship between the money supply and the economy. Just start with the proposition that the Federal Reserve is, after all, the bank of issue. Every time the Federal Reserve spends a dollar, it creates a dollar. The critical difference between the Fed and other types of financial institutions is that other types of financial institutions must first acquire a dollar in a deposit. A central bank labors under no such constraint.

I worked for the Federal Reserve for nearly seventeen years; every time it paid my salary, it was creating money, brand new money that never existed before (albeit, in very small amounts). So it does not really matter what the Fed buys: whether it is paying salaries or buying supplies for the office, whether it is buying Pepsi Cola bottle caps or bales of hay or government securities—it is creating brand new money.

The money the Fed creates is high-powered money in the sense that it forms the reserves in the banking system. The money supply that the Fed creates will affect the economy. It takes a little time, sometimes, but an increase in money will eventually result in an increase in spending; that increase in spending will deplete inventories; this will cause orders to go to the wholesalers, to the factories, and result in an increase in employment and hours worked. This will increase personal income, which will lead to further increases in spending and temporary increases in real gross domestic product.

If, on the other hand, the Federal Reserve has decided that it wants to follow a more restrictive monetary policy because it is concerned about inflation, then the Federal Reserve as the central bank can act as our main defense against inflation. It can act either by creating money at a slower rate, or by actually destroying money—and it can destroy money just as surely as it can create it. In doing so, it will temporarily slow the economy, but the problem with doing so is that the time periods during which these temporary effects take place are highly variable.

Milton Friedman is fond of saying that the fluctuations of money growth over the years have actually done more to create the ups and downs in the business cycle than have any natural events. Thus, the monetarists have a prescription. The monetarists' prescription is for slow, steady growth in the money supply. Slow in order to have little or no inflation. Steady in order not to create a disturbance in the real economy.

The above monetarist view worked well during the 1960s and 1970s, and even the first part of the 1980s. Since then, there have been problems; but the underlying truths of monetarism have not changed.

Conclusion

In conclusion, the following truths have not changed, but because of the changing financial scene, we no longer have the nice neat "laboratory" for demonstrating the effects of monetary actions:

1. The ultimate impact of monetary actions is on *nominal* magnitudes; i.e., GDP in current prices and nominal interest rates.
2. Short-run changes in money can impact real magnitudes; i.e., output and employment.
3. Therefore it follows that slow, steady growth in money is the best the Fed can do for the economy.
4. If the Fed's "best" is not good enough, look to fiscal (tax) policy to improve economic performance—actions that will improve productivity and real growth by encouraging capital formation.

Note

1. The reason I make the distinction between real resources and human resources is that countries that are very small and land-locked and do not have very much in the way of natural resources, like Switzerland, can nonetheless have very successful economies that enjoy good economic growth.

Part III

Operational Details

9

Peter D. Sternlight

The Implementation of Monetary Policy

When I came to the New York Fed's Research Department in 1950, Alan Holmes had been there for a couple of years. Incredible as it may seem, we were both in the Foreign Research Division—somewhat of a far cry from the open market operations arena where we both ended up. Perhaps even more astonishing, Alan Holmes had started out as a Russian expert—having come to the Bank after a stint at Columbia's Russian Institute. By the time I joined the Bank, though, in the British unit as it happens, Alan had switched over to be the Middle East expert—but really he was becoming an all-around utility infielder, as his talents became better known to the Bank's top management. That brought him in touch with foreign exchange operations, domestic desk operations, and various research positions at increasing levels of responsibility. I, like just about everyone at the Bank, had exceptionally high regard for Alan as the consummate professional.

My own path was a little different. After returning from military service, and notably after the famous Treasury–Federal Reserve Accord of 1951 that opened up scope for more meaningful use of domestic monetary policy, I was able to switch from foreign to domestic research for several years. During part of that time I was on loan to the Open Market Desk, helping to draft reports. That led, in time, to a permanent move to the open market area in 1961, where I have been ever since, except for a couple of years at the Treasury in the mid-1960s. I also did an earlier stint at Treasury for a few months in 1961, assisting Bob Roosa (undersecretary for Monetary Affairs). I followed Alan Holmes as manager of the System Account for Domestic Operations in 1979. Actually, it took two people to replace Alan because by that time he had been serving for a few years as manager of both the foreign and domestic operations desks at the New York Fed.

I have sometimes wondered how much at home, or otherwise, Alan might feel in the financial markets of the early 1990s. Certainly there are times and circumstances, such as dealing with the markets in the wake of the recent revelations of improper activities by a major securities firm, when I wish I could have a touch of his superb judgment in knowing how to respond. In some significant respects, though, while the markets have undergone change—including vast growth in size and development of new financial instruments—I think Alan would not find it terribly different trying to carry out Federal Reserve open market operations now from when he left the scene more than a decade ago. Then, as now, the central task was to serve as the balance wheel, the marginal provider or absorber of reserves in the banking system, in order to affect the climate for money and credit growth and, ultimately, the behavior of the economy, including employment and prices.

Rules versus Discretion

The particular techniques of operations have evolved over time, with changing degrees of emphasis on such elements as interest rates or various reserve measures. But I think there is more linkage than separation over time, and in fact our operational techniques have been known to circle back from time to time, returning to earlier haunts. A recurring theme in these cycles of trading desk techniques is the degree of discretion to be allowed in implementing policy from day to day, as opposed not to "indiscretion" but to pursuit of some sort of fixed rule such as a money supply or growth target. The tradition at the Fed's trading desk is to favor a sizable dollop of discretion—probably a natural inclination because it makes us seem less like robots responding mechanically to rules. The search or hunger for rules has tended to come more from the academic world, perhaps because some people in that quarter have a natural distrust of the foibles of merely human practitioners.

My problem with rigid rules, such as aiming at "X" percent money supply growth or reserve base growth, is that relationships can and do change in a dynamic economy—because of law, regulation, or custom. Indeed, many monetarists from the 1970s, who deplored with good reason the Fed's repeated overruns of its money growth objectives in that period, felt they had to abandon strict monetarism in the 1980s when relationships between standard money growth measures and the economy changed sharply to an extent that far surpassed our predictive abilities. Even after seeming to settle down a bit in more recent years, the relationships still seem too fragile now to steer our course with great confidence.

On the other hand, total "discretion" is not a totally satisfactory answer either. There have to be principles guiding that discretion and, hopefully, some capable people to exercise it. The underlying rules relate in my view to a process of working toward price stability, reasonable economic growth, and low unemployment. But the gap between these more ultimate economic objectives and our immediate focus on the day-to-day availability of bank reserves is so great that it can often be useful to have some intermediate objectives that concentrate on measures like money and credit growth.

The Objectives of Open Market Operations

With that background, I would like to describe what we do now with our open market operations, and what we think we are accomplishing. The immediate objective, as I have said, is to affect or "control" (depending on how omnipotent we want to sound) the availability of bank reserves. In a sense, the trading desk's job is to control the *non-borrowed* reserves—i.e., those other than what is borrowed at the discount window. But in a broader sense we are seeking to affect the nonborrowed reserves in order to influence the amount that needs to be borrowed—because that borrowed portion, or the gap in needs that tends to be filled by borrowing, is related to the degree of pressure or tension in the market for reserves. That degree of pressure exerts a major impact on the Fed funds rate, which is the overnight rate on bank reserves, and through that rate has an influence throughout the short-term money market and eventually the entire spectrum of interest rates. Banks do not like to turn to the discount window, even though the rate typically looks attractive. Their reluctance is a combination of not wanting to be chided by the Fed about overusing this facility, and not wanting to be perceived by the financial community as having to use the window, as it could be interpreted as a sign of weakness or distress. Digging still deeper, we seek to affect borrowing and tension in the bank reserves market in order to achieve the climate of reserve availability sought by the Federal Open Market Committee (FOMC)—

so as to bring about its objectives for money and credit growth and ultimately the desired growth pace and price performance of the economy.

Open market operations interface not only with the discount window but also with reserve requirements. Though changes in reserve requirement ratios are infrequent, the *framework* of reserve requirements—together with clearing balance needs—sets in place a *need* or demand for bank reserves. Deliberately, we supply fewer reserves than the banking system wants, knowing well that the difference will have to be covered at the discount window. Because of bank reluctance to borrow, the size of that difference, or borrowing gap, tends to determine the degree of pressure, and hence the rate level, in the federal funds market.

Going back a few years, we thought we could identify a fairly reliable relationship between the amount of borrowing we imposed on the banking system and the spread of the Fed funds rate over the discount rate. We had always been prepared for short-term deviations in such a relationship because borrowing serves as a short-run safety valve in case of unexpected reserve shortages that might emerge from a variety of factors, such as a bulge in the Treasury's balance at the Fed or a computer breakdown at a money center bank or Reserve Bank that disrupts normal flows of information, securities, or funds (see Figure 9.1). But we did think that over time a reasonably predictable pattern of behavior would show through to relate borrowing and the funds rate. The strength of that relationship has withered in the last few years. I am not prepared to say it has disappeared, but at best it has eroded. It still makes sense to expect a greater borrowing gap to be associated with a higher funds rate at a given discount rate, but the slope and intercepts of the line are uncertain. In practical terms that means we have to treat the borrowing levels in our reserve paths with some considerable flexibility; to put it another way, the erosion of that relationship tends to leave us more in the position of aiming for a funds rate in our day-to-date operations than we have liked to admit.

The Conduct of Open Market Policy

Open market policy in the United States is set by the FOMC, a body made up of the seven presidentially appointed governors on the Federal Reserve Board, and five of the twelve Reserve Bank presi-

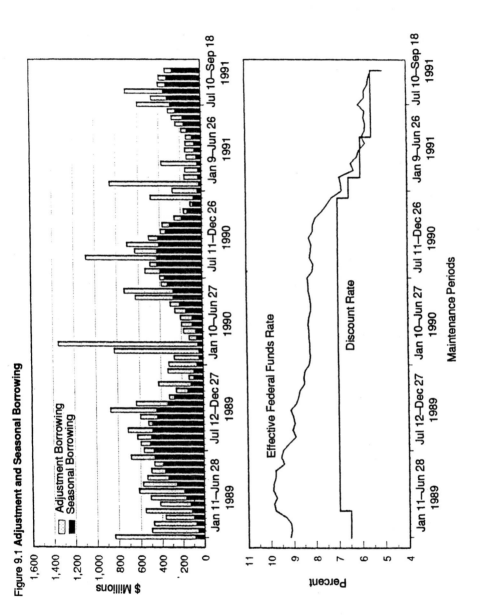

Figure 9.1 Adjustment and Seasonal Borrowing

dents. The New York Fed president is a permanent voting member while the other four serve in a planned rotation among the other eleven Banks. In this blend of centralized and regional interest, all the Reserve Bank presidents participate in the policy discussion. Only in the voting process itself is there a distinction. The meetings result in directives to the New York Fed to carry out operations—because the financial markets, and particularly the government securities market, are centered in New York.

In 1990 operations totaled about $500 billion, carried out with about forty primary dealers. The bulk of the operations are very short-term and self-reversing, designed to inject or extract reserves for a few days at a time. The total also includes about $25 billion of outright operations, intended to add or remove reserves on a more lasting basis. Given that the total reserve base on which we operate is just about $50 billion these days, the volume of operations may seem quite large, but the great bulk of what we do is merely offsetting short-run swings in various technical factors that affect reserve levels for a few days at a time. That does not demean the importance, including the potential policy significance, of such operations. On the contrary, it can be highly significant whether a technical reserve need is met promptly and generously or more sluggishly and reluctantly—this could spell the difference between policies of ease and restraint.

In their regular meetings, generally eight times yearly, the FOMC sets targets for monetary growth and desired conditions of reserve availability deemed to be consistent with underlying objectives for growth in the economy, progress toward price stability, and balanced international accounts. Annual targets for money growth are reviewed twice a year, in January and July, for presentation to Congress shortly following those meetings. Meanwhile, at those and other meetings the Committee frames its expectations for quarterly growth rates in these money measures. It also agrees on expected levels of discount window borrowings and Fed funds rates regarded as consistent with bringing about desired money growth and overall economic performance. The Committee directives to the New York Fed trading desk typically call for continuation, or a reduction or increase, in the degree of reserve pressure to be imposed, depending on whether policy is being held steady, eased, or tightened.

Latitude is generally provided for some modification in the degree of pressure as an intermeeting period proceeds, depending on factors such as strength of the economy, price developments, and monetary growth. That intermeeting leeway is essentially exercised by the chairman, with advice of senior staff, perhaps a comment from the account manager, and, depending on the extent of the change, possibly with intermeeting consultation of the whole Committee.

For example, the Directive adopted at the August 1991 meeting said:

> [T]he Committee seeks to maintain the existing degree of pressure on reserve positions. Depending upon progress toward price stability, trends in economic activity, the behavior of the monetary aggregates, and developments in foreign exchange and domestic financial markets, somewhat greater reserve restraint might, or somewhat lesser reserve restraint would be, acceptable in the intermeeting period.

The Directive then went on to indicate expected growth rates in the broad M_2 and M_3 money measures in coming months.

The Directive just cited is known as an "asymmetric" one. It called for no immediate change in policy, but in setting the stage for possible moves either to the accommodative or restrictive side it exhibited a leaning or bias to the easier side by using the words "would" or "might" in an appropriate context.

This particular Directive also illustrates something of the policy dilemma facing the Fed these days (1991) in trying to decide to which star one's wagon should be hitched. As shown in Figures 9.2 and 9.3, the broad M_2 and M_3 measures were distinctly soft, veering to the low end of the Committee's desired growth ranges. On the other hand, M_1, shown in Figure 9.4, was growing strongly. The Committee had decided some time before not to "target" M_1, because of lack of confidence in its relationship to economic activity, but policymakers have continued to look at it, and some have made more of it (and related reserve base growth) than others.

What does one do with such a mixture of signals? The Fed's response has been to weigh the information conveyed by the monetary aggregates alongside information on the real economy and price trends, while at the same time seeking to evaluate special factors that seem to be affecting the behavior of particular aggregates—such as the dampening of M_2 growth because of movements into bond funds, equities, or Treasury securities. Meantime M_3 has been specially

Figure 9.2 M₂: Levels and Targets (Cones and Tunnels)

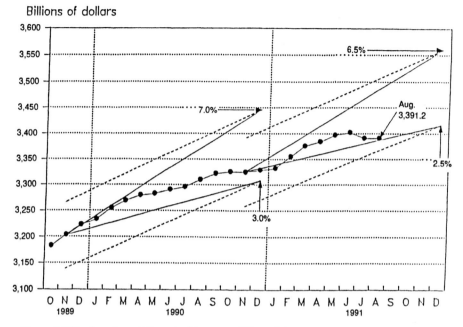

Figure 9.3 M₃: Levels and Targets (Cones and Tunnels)

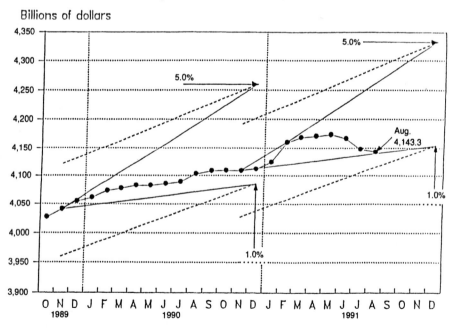

Figure 9.4 **M₁ Levels**

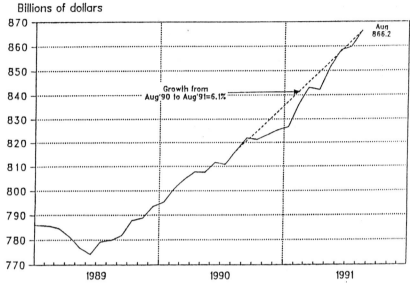

Billions of dollars

Growth from
Aug'90 to Aug'91=6.1%

Aug
866.2

1989   1990   1991

impacted by the collapse of the thrift institutions. If we just "explain away" the aggregates and look through to the real economy, are the aggregates of any real value? In my view, they are; analysis of their movements *has* made a difference in the timing and extent of recent policy moves, although I would have to acknowledge that the really preponderant weight behind policy moves has been on developments in real economic activity and the sense of greater progress regarding inflation.

Mechanics of Operations

In a day-to-day sense, the implementation of policy revolves around achieving a "reserve path." The path is constructed by projecting levels of required reserves for the current two-week reserve averaging period and the next couple of periods, adding an allowance for the banks' desire to hold excess reserves, and subtracting an allowance for discount window borrowing that is deemed consistent with the Committee's current Fed funds rate expectations. The funds rate "expectation" is essentially the measure of desired reserve pressure referenced in the Directive. Given the uncertain relationship between borrowing and the funds rate, the borrowing allowance is typically regarded with a considerable measure of flexibility. There is also flexibility in weighing the allowance for excess reserves, as demands can vary.

Each day, we are presented with new information on reserves that enables us to compare the projected level of actual nonborrowed reserves in the current reserve-averaging period with the "path" level derived as just described. This comparison gives rise to an indicated need to add or drain reserves in the current period in order to reach the path level of nonborrowed reserves. Reserves can be added or drained by buying or selling securities. At the same time, we can observe developments in the Fed funds market—the overnight market in bank reserves.

It is essentially an evaluation of the projected need to add or drain reserves, alongside the observation of the funds markets, that leads to the Trading Desk's daily decision to add or drain reserves, or perhaps do nothing on a particular day. Depending on the projected size and duration of a reserve need, the Desk might enter the market to buy securities on an outright basis, or perhaps inject reserves for a few days with repurchase agreements. Our market purchases are made on a competitive basis, with the group of primary dealers in government securities. If indications coming from the funds market seem to be inconsistent with projected reserve needs, an operation to add reserves might be modified or delayed. To do otherwise—for example, to add reserves aggressively when the funds market is soft, notwithstanding a projected reserve need—could convey a misleading signal of policy ease to the market. And that is something we would very much want to avoid.

Most of the time, fortunately, the signals from the money market are reasonably consistent with the reserve projections, enabling us to go about our task of adding or draining reserves without undue concern about giving unintended policy signals. At times, the information from the funds market might be a good tip-off that reserves are really more (or less) plentiful than projected, so that the modification of operations is entirely appropriate on reserve grounds as well. At other times, it may take a few days for a projected reserve need or excess to show through, and we just have to be a bit patient. On some occasions, our strong aversion to providing "wrong" policy signals has led us to drain reserves even though we projected a need for *more* reserves, just because of an easy funds market—or to add reserves when our projections show reserves above the path level, just because of an unduly tight money market.

The common thread in implementing open market operations is that what might seem like a fairly mechanical sort of operation is not that at all. Even the most routine daily decision requires an element of judgment in weighing the System's actions and the market's possible reactions to whatever we do or do not do on a particular day. This careful weighing of alternatives, including the need to think several moves ahead and factor in market reactions to our actions, was a skill that came naturally to Alan Holmes. It illustrates time and again the great debt owed by those privileged to have known and worked with him.

10

RICHARD V. ADAMS

Debt Management

Open market operations are the primary way in which the Fed conducts monetary policy. Since open market operations consist of the buying and selling of government debt, to understand the operation of monetary policy one must understand how the government securities market works. In this essay I describe the operation of one important player in the debt markets—the Treasury—and how it manages the government debt.

The U.S. government is in debt (1991) to the tune of $3.5 trillion. This debt has accumulated over the years because the revenues of the government have not been equal to the expenditures of the government—it is that simple. The consequences of this debt and the ongoing deficits and the accumulation of $3.5 trillion of debt have been the subject of much debate among economists, politicians, and concerned citizens, but that is not the topic of this essay. The subject here is technical: how that debt is managed so that new deficits are financed and old debt coming due is refinanced. Careful debt management is necessary so that government has the funds it needs when it needs them, and so that the cost of borrowing, in terms of interest, is held to a minimum.

Nonmarketable Debt

The government's debt consists of two general categories: marketable and nonmarketable. The nonmarketable securities are of three types: First there are the savings bonds that individuals buy. This debt is redeemable at par when it matures and interest is paid either periodically or at maturity.

A second category of nonmarketable securities is issued to government accounts themselves, such as the Social Security account. When you pay your Social Security taxes to the government, the government invests these funds in nonmarketable, special issues of Treasury securities. These do not trade; they just secure the government's Social Security receipts and they do, in fact, help to finance the government.

A third small category of nonmarketable debt is issued to state and local governments to enable them to employ funds temporarily. These three categories of nonmarketable debt total $1.2 trillion. Non-marketable debt is relatively easy to manage, and provides a comparatively stable source of finance. Nonmarketable debt has no important connection to Federal Reserve open market operations, which are conducted entirely by buying and selling marketable U.S. securities.

Marketable Debt

Marketable debt consists of three kinds of securities: Treasury bills, Treasury notes, and Treasury bonds. There are about $550 billion of Treasury bills outstanding; $1.33 trillion of Treasury notes; and $441 billion of Treasury bonds. Thus the total marketable debt of the United States is about $2.3 trillion. Treasury bills are short-term securities the Treasury sells to the public; they have maturities of one year or less. Bills are regularly issued in maturities of three months, six months, and one year. Treasury bills are sold at a discount—for example, 90 cents on the dollar—and at maturity, a year later, you get the face value back, giving a yield of 11 percent on an original 90 cents.

Treasury notes are issued in maturities of two to ten years. They are not issued at a discount, but at par, and pay interest each six months. If you buy a 10 percent Treasury note, you get interest of 5 percent each six months until maturity. At maturity, you get your principal back, which means the Treasury must get the cash to pay you by selling new debt, or by paying from its cash balance.

Treasury bonds are the same as notes, but are issued with maturities over ten years. Bonds, like notes, pay a stated interest rate in semiannual payments until maturity, at which time the original principal amount is repaid.

The Major Investors in Treasuries

Of the $2.3 trillion of marketable government securities outstanding, about $175 billion are owned by banks—a little less than 9 percent of the total. Insurance companies own $130 billion; state and local governments own $339 billion; foreigners own $392 billion; and a broad category of "other holders" owns almost $700 billion of these securities. This "others" category consists of private pension funds and mutual funds (other than money market funds, which are separate). Treasury ownership statistics have become less complete in recent years because of budget constraints; and the fact that "other holders" is a large category and not broken down by type of holder leaves a bit of a gap in our knowledge of the ownership of Treasury securities.

The ownership figures do suggest that practically every investor that owns fixed income securities has an interest in the U.S. Treasury securities market. Investors either hold them themselves, or are interested because this is the key market in the financial system and interest rates on every privately issued debt security are based on rates in the U.S. Treasury securities market. It is a market that everybody is involved in; a huge market with $125 billion a day in trading volume through "primary dealers" trading with their customers. This excludes the amounts that dealers trade among themselves through their brokers.

The market is efficient, in the classical sense. There are large numbers of buyers and sellers dealing with a homogeneous product; the participants all have the same information. All known information at a given point of time is reflected in market prices. Only new information makes market prices change; a new piece of economic news, new political news, a military event somewhere—anything that goes on in the world can affect the level and direction of prices and interest rates in the Treasury market.

The U.S. government has an interest in maximum market efficiency. The more efficient the market is, the better the prices the Treasury obtains for its securities.

The Term Structure of Federal Debt

When should securities be sold? They are sold when the Treasury needs funds, either for re-funding purposes or to raise new cash. As deficits have risen and accumulated in the last twenty years, this has necessitated a regularization of the issuance of Treasury securities. There is now a very precise schedule of Treasury debt offerings. Specifically, three- and six-month bills are issued weekly; one-year bills once a month; two- and five-year notes once a month; ten- and thirty-year maturities quarterly; seven-year maturities quarterly. Thus there is a regular schedule of issuing Treasury debt that is predictable in terms of the amount of money to be raised. And the way to raise more money is to add to the size of those regular offerings; or if the need for money is temporary, the Treasury will issue short-term bills called "cash management bills" to tide the Treasury over until it collects its taxes on April 15, June 15, or September 15. Again, the question of when Treasuries should be sold is just a matter of when the funds are needed. Under present heavy deficits, the Treasury's need for finance is more or less constant and a regular schedule of debt offerings is required.

What maturities should be sold? When you have small deficits and small debts, it is less important to completely regularize debt issuance. You can issue Treasury securities in parts of the market that seem attractive in terms of market demand. If the five-year maturities are in short supply in the market because investors have taken them all up and put them in portfolios, it might be a good idea to sell five-year maturities. Some other maturity might be attractive for some other specific reason. However, when you have a $300 billion deficit, and when there is $850 billion to re-fund annually, it is not practical to try issuing securities in various parts of the market that seem to be attractive. A regular and systematic schedule for the issuance of Treasury debt is prudent, predictable, and nondisruptive to the market.

The question of the maturity of the debt also has a bearing on the debt management. When I was at the Treasury, the average maturity of the Treasury debt was two years. We were concerned about this because it meant a very heavy re-funding schedule on top of a large amount of new money needed to finance the government's deficit. There were too many entries to the market by the Treasury to borrow money. It became difficult to coordinate Treasury financing with financing of the other federal agencies that were also heavy borrowers. The market for corporate debt would also be affected at times from this congestion. So there was a need to extend the maturity of the Treasury debt. Over the years since 1970, the Treasury has been able to extend the average maturity of marketable debt to about five years. This has been accomplished through regular issuance of long-term securities in larger and larger volume.

Aside from the housekeeping problem, the proper maturity structure of the debt has been the subject of much debate on the part of economists and academics for years. Some believe that federal debt management policies have little or nothing to do with economic stabilization. For that matter, many economists do not believe that federal fiscal policy is a good stabilization tool either. These observers believe that Federal Reserve monetary policy is the important macroeconomic policy tool and therefore what the debt managers do will have no particular bearing on economic activity. The solution from this point of view is that the Treasury should stay out of the way of the Fed by regularizing the debt schedule—and that is essentially what the Treasury debt managers have done.

Another view is that the Treasury should emphasize or even concentrate on Treasury bills. They argue that the Treasury bill rate is almost always the lowest rate in the market and massive amounts of interest could be saved if the Treasury concentrated on the short-term market. Furthermore, they argue that a large short-term debt would impose a discipline on the government to avoid inflationary policies. A rise in the short-term rate brought on by rising inflation would rapidly affect Treasury borrowing costs. This in turn would have an adverse impact on the federal budget and impinge on the implementation of government economic and social policy: such prospects should serve as a deterrent to inflationary government policies.

The problem with this idea is that there does not seem to be any evidence that government policy is influenced by interest costs or fear of inflation until the body politic becomes alarmed, and by that time the damage has been done. I doubt that the discipline imposed on the government by selling Treasury bills only would result in any savings at all. Another problem with "bills only" involves federal budgeting. For example, an increase in short-term interest rates beyond what had been budgeted could cause a substantial rise in outlays—throwing the government into a deeper deficit. As a practical matter, the Treasury will need to continue to tap a wide range of maturities in order to finance the huge ongoing deficits.

What Features Should Treasury Bonds Have?

Another set of reform proposals has concerned what, if any, special features Treasury issues should have. U.S. Treasury securities are the highest quality securities in the world. This stems from the size, the strength, and the power of the U.S. economy. In owning Treasury securities, there is no question of security in terms of timely return of the principal or receiving your interest on time. The issue here is that with securities as strong and safe as U.S. Treasuries, why would it be necessary or desirable to add any special features to make them more salable? There have been some experiments in the postwar years with callable issues and extendable issues, but currently the Treasury sticks to the concept of fixed rates, fixed maturities, noncallable securities issued on a regular schedule. With very few exceptions, the Treasury sticks to the traditional types of securities. There are some thirty-year bonds that the Treasury can call after twenty-five years. That is a call feature that does not cost the Treasury very much because it is not worth very much at the outset. However, even this low-cost feature has been discontinued in recent years. There have also been proposals to tie the interest rate on Treasury bonds to the CPI, or to some other inflation indicator. Treasury bonds backed by gold have also been proposed. Some people want the Treasury to issue zero coupon bonds; others want them to issue put options or extension options. The Treasury has resisted these ideas, believing that U.S. securities are attractive just as they are. Additional features would probably increase rather than reduce borrowing costs. As far as inflation-indexed issues are concerned, the Treasury has so far not been willing to concede on the inflation fight by issuing indexed paper.

The Federal Debt Management Policy Team

The federal debt management policy team, which manages the Treasury's entries to the market, is headed by the secretary of the Treasury. The undersecretary for Domestic Finance has the responsibility for debt management; under that level is the assistant secretary for Domestic Finance; and under them, the deputy assistant secretary for Domestic Finance. The deputy assistant secretary is the line officer for Treasury debt management. This official does the planning for the sale of Treasury securities, conducts liaison with the market, and keeps close, constant track of market conditions.

The task of the debt manager is to issue new bills, notes, or bonds to pay off maturing securities and to raise new money for the government as needed. This is accomplished by selling securities to the public.

Now let us recap the issues in Treasury debt management. We have said that the debt managers must be able to raise money when the Treasury needs it: they have to raise money for re-funding mature issues, they have to raise new money for government outlays. The Treasury therefore must borrow frequently and systematically in order to be efficient in tapping the market.

There is a $348 billion deficit looming in the current fiscal year (1992). That means that the total issuance in this fiscal year will amount to a staggering $1.2 trillion. This will include $850 billion of re-funding. That means that the Treasury is going to be very active in the market, and it will have to accomplish its financing task in a way that will be least disruptive to financial markets in general.

The issues that the Treasury is going to have to confront are: how can securities be sold, when should they be sold, what maturities should be sold, and what special features should these securities have—that is, what enhancements should they have to make them more attractive, if any.

The Market Structure

The structure of the Treasury market is important because the market is the forum in which the Treasury and the debt management officials operate. The Treasury securities market is an over-the-counter market—there is no central exchange like the New York Stock Exchange in which to deal with these securities.

The core of the Treasury market consists of thirty-nine primary dealers in U.S. government securities, mostly located in New York. This group includes the big bond houses that most of us have heard of: Salomon, Merrill Lynch, Goldman Sachs, Morgan Guaranty, Morgan Stanley.

A recognized primary dealer can trade hundreds of millions of dollars of Treasury securities instantly by telephone and does so each day. Transactions take place between dealers, between dealers and brokers, and between dealers and their customers. This is the Treasury securities market that was in the news in the early 1990s because of the Salomon Brothers scandal wherein important rules of the business were broken.

The primary dealers are recognized and supervised by the Federal Reserve System. They are the dealers that the Federal Reserve System uses when it executes monetary policy. One of the ways the Federal Reserve controls the supply of money and credit is to buy and sell U.S. government securities in the market. The Fed does this through the thirty-nine primary dealers. When the Federal Reserve System enters the market to buy securities to supply banking system reserves, it calls around to the dealers and asks them to make offers. A dealer offers what it wishes to sell and the Federal Reserve buys as much as it needs in order to do whatever it has to do at the lowest prices offered. In the simplest terms, this is how Federal Reserve open market operations are conducted.

In order to maintain their status as primary dealers, dealers must maintain both a certain share of the trading volume of the market and at least $50 million of capital, and they are required to report their positions and trading activity daily to the Federal Reserve Bank of New York. They must make markets in Treasury securities in all maturities. They must also submit to regulation and supervision by the Fed.

In return for assuming market-making responsibilities and submitting to regulation and supervision by the Fed, primary dealers are the only ones the Fed uses to execute its monetary policy. Being a primary dealer, therefore, has been considered to be an important and valuable franchise. Many investment firms and investment institutions prefer to deal only with Treasury dealers who are primary dealers, recognized by the Fed.

Being a primary dealer is also considered a matter of prestige in the market, and a primary dealer may feel it has an advantage by being directly in touch with the Treasury and in contact with the Treasury more regularly than others might be. This contact might provide some market insight that others do not have, and it may give primary dealers a slight edge in relationships with major customers and major institutional investors.

While the primary dealers constitute the core of the Treasuries market, there is a small "sub-core" group of brokers in government securities—about four or five companies that are relatively unknown outside the industry. These firms perform the brokerage function between primary dealers. One of the things that makes this primary dealer group an inside club is that its members are the only ones that can trade with these brokers. So if a Merrill Lynch trader wants to buy $100 million worth of Treasury bills, the trader does not go directly to a Morgan Stanley trader, for example, and voice his or her desire to buy the Treasury bills. The Merrill Lynch trader does not wish to reveal an interest to the Morgan Stanley trader since the Morgan Stanley trader might somehow gain an advantage. A broker is used to bring Merrill together with another anonymous dealer who wishes to sell the bills. Neither party knows who is on the other side of the trade except that it is another of the primary dealers.

The Salomon Brothers Treasury market scandal of 1991 raises questions about the structure of the market and market practices. In 1991, in bidding for a number of Treasury issues, Salomon Brothers broke a rule that limits to 35 percent the amount of a new issue a single bidder can bid for. The result was that Salomon in several instances wound up owning—or controlling—very large percentages of some new issues; in one case, up to 95 percent of the issue.

The reason the Fed will not allow more than 35 percent of an issue to be bid for by one bidder is that by controlling an issue, one can "squeeze" buyers. By controlling a security, one can name the price, and the buyer either pays it or does not get the securities. There is also the possibility that a controlling dealer could compound the violation by squeezing the financing market. Short sellers could be forced to pay exorbitant cost to acquire securities to deliver against their short sales. If you are on the wrong side of such a situation, you get hurt in two ways. You get hurt on the price of the security you are short, and/or you get hurt in borrowing scarce securities to deliver against a short position.

The upshot of this complicated case is that because of Salomon Brothers' irregular activities, the market for U.S. government securities was, at times in 1991, distorted and not functioning efficiently. An uneven playing field existed and some participants experienced unnecessary losses. The public's confidence in the market was shaken, and questions were raised about the nature and scope of government regulation of this crucial financial market.

Some Issues Relevant to Reform

How should the securities of the U.S. Treasury be sold? This is a subject of frequent discussion among those interested in this market, and it has been sharpened by the Salomon Brothers situation, which raised questions about the methods and techniques of selling Treasury securities. Since 1971, the Treasury has used the auction method to sell securities. It has always auctioned bills, but beginning in 1971 the Treasury began to auction its notes and bonds. Previously the practice had been for the Treasury to put a price on the securities it wanted to sell, setting the amount of securities it wanted to sell, and then hoping that the public would subscribe. In order to be sure that the sale would succeed, the Treasury had to set a price cheap enough to make sure the public would buy the issue in sufficient quantity. That cost the Treasury money, a lot of money—probably about a 0.125 percent concession in order to make sure that the offerings were successful.

The auction technique improved the situation dramatically. The Treasury set the amount of securities it wanted to sell and the market set the price. At a price determined by competitive bidding, the securities were going to find a buyer. Bidding is done in terms of yield, and the Treasury accepts bids starting at the lowest yield, continuing until all the securities are covered. At that point, an average bid yield is calculated, and limited amounts are awarded to bidders at the average of the accepted competitive bids. That is basically the way the Treasury securities auctions are handled. In 1992, however, the Treasury started experimenting with another auctioning technique.

The new type of auction the Treasury is trying is a single-price or "Dutch auction." In a Dutch auction, instead of auctioning securities and awarding them at different prices, taking the lowest yields first and then awarding at higher yields until all securities are sold, the Treasury simply awards all the securities at a single price—the lowest price accepted in the competitive bidding process. This may sound strange at first, awarding securities at the *lowest* bid. But here we have a case where economic theory impacts policy. The economic theory behind the Dutch auction tells us that if bidders do not have to worry about paying a higher price than other bidders, they will be more likely to participate in auctions and perhaps to bid higher prices. At least if this method encourages broader participation in Treasury auctions, market efficiency will be enhanced.

In the conventional auction, securities can be awarded at or just slightly above the lowest accepted price. The skillful bidder has a considerable advantage over those who bought securities at higher prices. Market participants do not like to be in such a position and they may feel uncomfortable about participating and leave the auction "game" to the primary dealers. The Dutch auction is designed to encourage participation. If A thinks an issue is worth a 7.00 percent yield and B thinks it is worth 6.95 percent, while C thinks it is worth 7.05 percent, in a Dutch auction B puts her bid in at 6.95 percent because she is happy with that rate, but with the others bidding 7.00 percent and 7.05 percent the securities might be awarded as low as 7.05 percent and all the securities would then be awarded at that rate. B will be delighted—she got the securities cheaper than she expected and she does not have to worry about others owning the securities cheaper.

The Dutch auction has been tried a couple of times in the past, but it was discontinued because the secretary of the Treasury felt that it was not clear that the Treasury was saving any money. There is now another reason why the Treasury has resurrected the Dutch auction: it levels the playing field. The dealers like to think that their expertise and their knowledge of the market, their knowledge of customer interest, government finance, Federal Reserve policy, and all kinds of things they do to prepare themselves for auctions give them an edge. The reason for their success over the years, the reason they want to be primary dealers, is based on the perception that because of their position in the market they are a little smarter than others.

Why should the primary dealers have this real or perceived advantage? As the market has evolved in recent years, that dealer's edge has been eroded mainly through widening access to information. A move toward the single-price auction will further reduce the primary dealer's edge. This, together with theoretical advantages in the single-price auction, has led the Treasury to adopt use of it in two- and five-year note auctions. Success here will lead to further use of this method.

A more radical proposal for selling Treasury debt was made in congressional testimony by Jack Bennett in 1990. Bennett was the undersecretary for Monetary Affairs in the mid-1970s and a proponent of the Dutch auction. Now, taking things a bit further, he says the ultimate goal for the Treasury should be to make its own market via electronic screens all over the world that would continuously offer prices at which the Treasury buys or sells its own securities. The Treasury would operate in large multiples, tailoring its activities to its cash requirements, market conditions, and numerous other factors that could affect policy. The point of Bennett's proposal is that Treasury securities should be handled by the Treasury; if you want to buy or sell Treasuries, go to the Treasury. Why should the Treasury have other people handling purchases and sales of its securities?

Bennett's proposal is unlikely to be followed up on in the foreseeable future. Too many private sector interests would be affected. There is also the problem of the Treasury having to establish a very sophisticated, high-powered worldwide group of people to handle the market. It would take a big operation and a lot of talent to handle it. Such a plan would also run counter to the current tendency toward privatization that seems to be occuring around the world. Thus, for the foreseeable future, changes in debt management seem likely to focus on changes in the auction technique, automating the bidding process and tinkering with the maturity structure of the debt.

Regulatory Reforms

Finally, another set of reform proposals has concerned who should regulate the government securities market. Currently, the Federal Reserve Bank of New York acts as the fiscal agent for the Treasury and handles the clearing of Treasury securities and the book entry system. If you buy a Treasury security you get an entry on the books of the Federal Reserve Bank of New York. The New York Fed also handles the Treasury auctions for the Treasury, along with supervising and monitoring the market. The Treasury makes the rules and the Federal Reserve Bank of New York enforces them. The regulation of the market has been reasonably strict but not very formal. The rules and regulations are not encoded into law, but it has been effective, at least until the Salomon Brothers scandal.

In the aftermath of the Salomon situation there has been a question of what agencies should regulate the Treasury securities market. The Federal Reserve did well informationally but perhaps the SEC should be given regulatory oversight. Apart from some cases of fraud, the SEC has not had a hand in the regulation of the Treasury securities market; now it wants to become involved. In considering such proposals in the wake of Salomon Brothers there was a possibility that Congress or the SEC would overreact and impose unnecessary, undesirable rules on the Treasury market. Historically, this market has been quite free and unregulated and therefore one of the most efficient markets anywhere. Imposing heavy-handed regulations would reduce efficiency and increase the cost of financing the government. Fortunately, the threat of unnecessary regulation of the U.S. government securities market seems to have receded. Continued surveillance is, however, necessary.

Conclusion

To the art of monetary policy, Treasury debt management has only a small contribution to make. However, at the level of practical market and financial policy, the way the U.S. government handles its budget, its debt, and its approach to the financial markets is of major importance to the economy. Debt management encompasses a wide range of economic and market disciplines, and the country has been fortunate over the years in having a long line of thoughtful, skillful people in both the public and private sectors formulating and guiding the government's financial policies. Alan Holmes was one of these distinguished leaders.

11

DEWEY DAANE

The Federal Open Market Committee in Action

The monetary policy process—how monetary policy gets put together—is not simply a reflection of the economic circumstances surrounding decisions, both domestic and international, and how policy should react to those circumstances. It is also, and importantly so, a reflection of the leadership in the Federal Reserve System, in particular the chairman of the Federal Reserve Board, and of the perspectives of the policy participants—both the Federal Reserve Board Members and the various Reserve Bank presidents.

Before plunging into my subject, "The Federal Open Market Committee in Action," I will describe what goes on in the very large, ornate Board Room at the Federal Reserve Board in Washington, a room complete with huge marble fireplace (albeit cracked), overhanging chandelier, and an impressive Board table (more impressive in my day than today!).

I want to emphasize that the process begins long before the assembly in the Board Room. It involves immense preparation, practically continuous, at the Reserve Banks and the Federal Reserve Board. In specific preparations, at each of the Reserve Banks, and at the Federal Reserve Board, there are lengthy briefings in the week or weeks preceding the FOMC meeting, involving intensive discussions by the policymakers with their respective staffs.

In connection with the advance preparations, and the meeting itself, there are three books, each with a different colored cover, that are an integral part of the preparation and the decision-making process. Sometimes, and not totally inaccurately, monetary policy is equated with these three books, which contain the essential information used in the formulation of monetary policy:

1. **The Beige Book**, in which each district collects and collates the regional evidence of significance and which then goes to all participants in advance of a meeting.

2. **The Green Book**, which embodies the Federal Reserve Board staff's compendium and analysis of all available domestic and international evidence that is relevant. This, too, is available in advance and used by all participants and its forecasts discussed at the meetings.

3. **The Blue Book**, which is really the operative document—typically setting forth three alternatives for action and the implications of each for financial conditions and the economy. The alternatives are (a) easier, (b) status quo, or (c) tighter policy prescriptions translated into specific figures, namely the federal funds rate and money supply growth. This book, usually received by policymakers on the weekend before the regular meeting, is the center of the policy discussion at the meeting itself.

The information in these books provides reasoned reflections on economic circumstances and discussion of how policy should react to these circumstances. The books provide the analytic background of the meetings; they guide and structure the discussions at the meetings, but do not determine monetary policy, and the meetings can sometimes take on a life of their own, departing from the prepared structure.

The FOMC in Action

At this point, come with me to the FOMC and let us make the heroic abstraction of mentally transporting ourselves to the Federal Reserve Board Room on a given Tuesday, about eight times a year.

At these meetings there are from forty to fifty individuals, consisting of Committee members and Committee staff. The actual Committee itself consists of twelve voting members. The voting members are the seven governors of the Federal Reserve Board, the president of the New York Federal Reserve, and, on a rotating basis, four of the other eleven presidents of Federal Reserve Banks. The other seven nonvoting presidents attend and participate in the discussions. The staff consists of staff members of the Federal Reserve Board and of the various Federal Reserve Banks. Monetary policy is formalized at these FOMC meetings, which constitute the most important part of the process and are therefore the center of discussion in this essay.

A Typical Meeting

Now let's try to follow a typical agenda. Exhibit 1 is a sample agenda constructed by Ann-Marie Meulendyke of the New York Federal Reserve Bank.[1]

Exhibit 1. Federal Open Market Committee Meeting Sample Agenda

1. Approval of minutes of actions taken at the last meeting of the Federal Open Market Committee
2. Foreign currency operations*
   A. Report on operations since the last meeting
   B. Action to ratify transactions since that meeting
3. Domestic open market operations*
   A. Report on operations since the last meeting
   B. Action to ratify transactions since that meeting
4. Economic situation
   A. Staff report on economic situation
   B. Committee discussion
5. Longer-run ranges for monetary policy (February and July meetings)
   A. Staff comments
   B. Committee discussion on longer-run ranges
   i. Review of ranges for year in progress
   ii. Establishment of tentative ranges for following year (July meeting)
6. Current monetary policy and domestic policy directive
   A. Staff comments
   B. Committee discussion
   C. Action to adopt directive
7. Confirmation of date for next meeting

Since the specific content of discussion under each topic often becomes quickly outdated by events, my review in this essay will simply

---

*At the February and July meetings, reports on operations in foreign currencies and the domestic securities market and their discussion are sometimes deferred until after the target rate ranges are developed, although this has not happened for a number of years.

generalize as to the nature of each item, giving a generic description rather than attempting a topical illustration that could so shortly become dated and no longer necessarily relevant.

Agenda

1. **Approval of minutes** of actions taken at the last meeting of the Federal Open Market Committee.

   This is self-explanatory and largely pro forma. Currently, the minutes include a summary of the economic and financial information available to the Committee at the meeting and contain a summary of the discussion of economic developments and monetary policy at the meeting.

2. **Foreign Currency Operations**
   A. Following approval of the minutes, all such meetings begin with a report from the Manager for Foreign Operations, System Open Market Account, in which he or she would have reviewed the course of the dollar over the intermeeting period in the foreign exchange market as well as any official intervention that might have taken place. The Manager may also review any new indebtedness of various countries or any new economic trends or developments in major industrial countries with implications for domestic policy, such as a slowdown in economic activity in Europe.
   B. Following this report and discussion, actions taken would be ratified. The report itself involves few surprises since it supplements daily and weekly reports circulated in between meetings to all participants as to conditions in the foreign exchange markets and any actions taken.

3. **Domestic Open Market Meetings**
   The review of foreign operations would be followed by a report from the Manager for Domestic Operations, System Open Market Account. He or she would make a detailed report on what actions had been taken in the market in implementing the domestic policy directive issued to the Federal Reserve Bank of New York at the previ-

ous meeting of the FOMC. For example, that directive could have suggested "maintaining the existing degree of pressure" on reserves with qualifications, for instance suggesting that "somewhat greater" or "slightly greater" or "somewhat lesser" or "slightly lesser" action in either direction "might," "could," or "would" be acceptable.

The nuances of the governing words determine whether or not the directive is "symmetric" or "asymmetric," meaning that it would be more or less acceptable for the Trading Desk to move in a given direction. In current practice, the chairman would make the decision for any change. Exhibit 2 shows sample directives, in this case both of an asymmetric directive (Directive A) and a symmetric directive (Directive B).

Exhibit 2. An Asymmetric and a Symmetric Directive

Directive A (Asymmetric Directive, November 17, 1992)

In the implementation of policy for the immediate future, the Committee seeks to maintain the existing degree of pressure on reserve positions. In the context of the Committee's long-run objectives for price stability and sustainable economic growth, and giving careful consideration to economic, financial, and monetary developments, slightly greater reserve restraint might, or slightly lesser reserve restraint would, be acceptable in the intermeeting period. The contemplated reserve conditions are expected to be consistent with growth of M_2 and M_3 over the period from September through December at annual rates of about 3.5 and 1 percent, respectively.

Votes for this action: Messrs. Greenspan, Corrigan, Angell, Hoenig, Kelley, Lindsey, Mullins, Ms. Phillips, and Mr. Syron.

Votes against this action: Messrs. Jordan, LaWare, and Melzer.

Directive B (Symmetric Directive, February 2 and 3, 1993)

In the implementation of policy for the immediate future, the Committee seeks to maintain the existing degree of pressure on reserve positions. In the context of the Committee's long-run objectives for price stability and sustainable economic growth, and giving careful consideration to economic, financial, and monetary developments, slightly greater reserve restraint or slightly lesser reserve restraint would be acceptable in the intermeeting period. The contemplated reserve conditions are expected to be consistent with little change in M_2 and M_3 over the period from January to March.

The Vote For:
Unanimous.

In Directive A, the nuances suggest that a move toward ease would be acceptable. In Directive B, the suggestion is that a move in *either* direction would be acceptable. The Committee would then take action to ratify the domestic transactions in the market covering the period since the last meeting of the Committee. Again, this ratification is of transactions already reported daily to all participants in between meetings.

4. Economic Situation

The FOMC would then turn its attention to the economic situation, first as seen by the staff and then as the individual members of the Committee see it.

As a backdrop for that discussion a key Federal Reserve Board staff adviser, currently Michael Prell, the director of the Federal Reserve Board's Division of Research, would review all the developments in terms of the staff's economic information and analysis. Then all the Committee members would enter into discussion and express their views—all members come to the meetings with their own forecasts and the Bank presidents in their remarks generally include the latest regional developments with implications for the national economy

Perhaps the chairman might outline his views first, although this practice would not be invariable with all chairmen. For example, my own experience is that Chairman Martin normally gave his own views last, while Chairman Burns laid out his views on the economy and on policy (in a general way) at the beginning. Chairman Volcker may also have followed that practice, while Chairman Greenspan instead may choose to offer his views on the economy and, again in a general way, on policy after the economic discussion but before the start of the monetary policy discussion. Assuming the chairman does elect to speak first, all policymakers would then feel free to enter into the dialogue. As to the Reserve Bank presidents, the Cleveland Federal Reserve Bank president, for example, might include comments on the foundries and basic industries; the Chicago Federal Reserve Bank president on the auto industry; the Kansas City president on the agricultural situation and the farmers' problems. The St. Louis president frequently brings a monetarist view and position to the table, so he may focus on the growth rates of M_2 and M_3 and their implications. But all the various members would make clear their agreement or disagreement with the staff analysis in the Green Book and their views as to the national economic outlook.

5. **Longer-Run Ranges for Monetary Policy (February and July Meetings)**

Prefatory to discussion by the Committee, Donald Kohn, director of the Board's Division of Monetary Affairs, would lead off with a briefing relative to the Blue Book, which for the February and July meetings contains alternative sets of ranges for Committee consideration (and discussions of the implications of those ranges).

At meetings when the Committee establishes its long-run ranges for growth of the money and debt aggregates in February and July, the Committee members and the nonvoting Federal Reserve Bank presidents prepare projections of economic activity and the rate of unemployment and inflation for the calendar year (at the February meeting). As indicated above, all of the policymakers at the meeting engage in extended discussions of the various factors underlying their outlooks for economic activity, inflation, and employment. In February and July those forecasts and the central tendencies are incorporated in the chairman's testimony and the Federal Reserve Board's report to the Congress under the Full Employment and Balanced Growth Act of 1978 (Humphrey–Hawkins). For illustrative purposes, the Economic Projections for 1993 made in February 1993 are shown in Table 11.1.

Table 11.1

Economic Projections for 1993

Measure		1992 Actual	FOMC Members and Other FRB Presidents	
			Range	Central Tendency
Percentage change, fourth quarter to fourth quarter	Nominal GDP	5.4	5.25 to 6.25	5.50 to 6
	Real GDP	2.9	2.50 to 4	3 to 3.25
	Consumer price index[a]	3.1	2.50 to 3	2.50 to 2.75
Average level in the fourth quarter—percent:	Unemployment rate[b]	7.3	6.50 to 7	6.75 to 7

[a] CPI for all urban consumers.
[b] Percentage of the civilian labor force.

Against the background of their economic review and forecasts, in February and July the Committee, as indicated, discusses the money growth developments and selects the ranges for monetary policy for the calendar year (or in July for the next year). Again, for illustrative purposes the ranges chosen in February 1993 for 1993 are shown in Table 11.2.

6. **Current Monetary Policy and Domestic Policy Directive**

A. Staff comments. It is at this point that the meeting turns to the actual consideration of what monetary policy will be followed. Prefatory to the discussions by the Committee, Donald Kohn would present the alternatives (usually three) as summarized in the Blue Book, including implications for financial markets and the economy of an easier, tighter, or status quo policy alternative, and would respond to questions or comments.

B. Committee discussions. Since the February 2–3, 1993, meeting of the FOMC was preparatory to meeting the Humphrey–Hawkins reporting requirements, the chairman's testimony of February 19, 1993, and the minutes of that February meeting, released on March 26, 1993, contain valuable insights as to the course of the Committee's discussions. In summary, the Committee noted the strengthening of the economy as reflected,

Table 11.2

Ranges of Growth of Monetary and Credit Aggregates (percentage change, fourth quarter to fourth quarter)

	1991	1992	1993
M2	2.5 to 6.5	2.5 to 6.5	2 to 6
M3	1 to 5	1 to 5	.5 to 4.5
Debt	4.5 to 8.5	4.5 to 8.5	4.5 to 8.5

among other things, in consumer spending (strong retail sales), sharply rising business spending for durable equipment, increasing outlays for housing, and a general improvement in business and consumer confidence. Most members expected additional moderation of inflation.

C. Action to adopt directive. Again, at this point, the chairman might reiterate his views as to the appropriate course of policy actions and the corresponding directive. There was obvious unanimity at the February meeting. All members endorsed a proposal to maintain unchanged conditions in reserve markets and all indicated they could accept a directive that did not incorporate any presumption with regard to the likely direction of possible intermeeting adjustments to policy (i.e., a symmetric directive). Concern was expressed over recent weakness in monetary aggregates; some commented that further easing might adversely affect inflation sentiment and interest rates; a few referred to a recent firming in commodity prices and a possible inflation updrift over the next few years.

By unanimous vote the Committee adopted a domestic policy directive including the following key paragraph:

In the implementation of policy for the immediate future, the Committee seeks to maintain the existing degree of pressure on reserve positions. In the context of the Committee's long-run objectives for price stability and sustainable economic growth, and giving careful consideration to economic, financial, and monetary developments, slightly greater reserve restraint or slightly lesser reserve restraint would be acceptable in the intermeeting period. The contemplated reserve conditions are expected to be consistent with little change in M2 and M3 over the period from January to March.

Implementation of FOMC Policy

The above final operative paragraph from the *February* meeting was not made pubic until March 26, the Friday *after* the *March* meeting of the Committee. It called for maintaining existing reserve pressures. How is this done? If the Committee wants to maintain existing reserve pressures, how does this come about?

Here I will have to ask you once again to make a heroic logistical abstraction and move from the Board Room on the second floor in the Federal Reserve Board building at 20th and Constitution in Washington, D.C., to the eighth floor of the Federal Reserve Bank of New York at 33 Liberty Street, New York, and its Trading Room, which is a large, almost square, corner room equipped with tables with turrets for each of the traders. There are about fifteen or sixteen traders who deal with about forty government security dealers; the manager of the System Open Market Account directs this activity.

Under operating procedure, their actions and reactions really revolve around bank reserves, the components of reserves, and what they know, or think they know, about reserves. Total bank reserves can be viewed in two ways.

$$TR = RR + ER = \text{Bank Demand for Reserves}$$
$$TR = NBR - BR = \text{F. R. Supply of Reserves,}$$

where

TR = Total reserves	TR = Total reserves
RR = Required reserves	NBR = Nonborrowed reserves
ER = Excess reserves	BR = Borrowings from Federal Reserve

Since excess reserves are fairly small and fairly constant (say, $1 billion), and required reserves might be calculated to be about $50 billion (calculated on a two-week average of deposits), this would yield a total Bank Demand for Reserves of some $51 billion. On the TR supply side we could assume that the same $51 billion of total reserves broke down into net borrowed reserves of $50 billion and $1 billion of member bank borrowing, which would be moderately restrictive.

Now assume that bank demand for reserves rises and required reserves goes up by $1 billion. Then the Fed Trading Desk can choose either to meet that demand by supplying another billion dollars of nonborrowed reserves, or it can force the banks to borrow at the discount window—which would be very restrictive indeed.

If the Trading Desk decides to supply reserves—and decisions are made daily by around 11:15 A.M.—this means that about 11:30 A.M. it would begin as nearly simultaneously as possible to contact all the U.S. government securities dealers and take offers at a price and then accept up to $1 billion needed in this example on a best-price basis. They have a further choice as to whether to buy the securities outright or on a repurchase basis, which would put a string on the reserves. However, the magnitudes of temporary RP operations range from about $1.5 billion (consistent with the example) to much higher amounts ($10 to $12 billion). Outright purchases are only done six or seven times a year, in magnitudes ranging from $2 billion to $12 billion. Presumably, the Fed funds rate would remain unchanged, consistent with the maintenance of existing reserve pressures. But in essence, and simplistically, this is how the process works. For a summary, see Table 11.3.

Concluding Comments

My conclusion will be short. Conceptually, central bank policy and practice more nearly resemble a living, changing, dynamic organism than a static system. Whether the changes from the "olden days" represent an improved and more effective central bank policy and mechanism is still, in my mind, an open question. The more mechanistic and quantitative approach does not necessarily appeal to a nonmathematical economist like me. In the end, it still, however, seems to me to rest on a judgment currently as to what Fed funds rate and level of bank borrowing from the Federal Reserve are consistent with the degree of restraint appropriate to the desired contour of the economy.

Someone has described a central banker as one who "fears someone in the world might be happy." As an ex-central banker, I can only hope that my description of the FOMC in action is still reasonably current and has not made too many of you unhappy by not giving a more colorful account of the personalities that make the process come to life. One of those personalities was Alan Holmes, who managed the System Open Market Account superbly for more than a decade from April 1965 until late 1979. Alan had great technical knowledge but, even

Table 11.3

The Monetary Policy Process

Formulation of Policy

A. Choice of money and debt annual growth ranges
    FOMC: February and July meetings

B. Specifications to Manager of Domestic Open Market Account
    1. Short-run money targets—M_2 and M_3
    2. Indications of federal funds rate (discuss in FOMC)
    3. Initial assumption for discount window borrowing
    FOMC: each of 8 meetings per year

C. Selection of discount rate
    Boards of Directors of Reserve Banks subject to Board approval

Implementation of Policy

A. Estimates of demand and supply of nonborrowed reserves
    Board and New York's Staff: daily

B. Review of demand and supply of nonborrowed reserves and money market
    conditions
    Account Manager: daily and biweekly

C. Execution of open market operations
    Account Manager: daily

more important, the intuition and judgment and sensitivity to the view of others that enabled him to satisfy nineteen diverse policy participants that he was indeed carrying out their individual and collective desires as to appropriate policy. One quick illustration that I recall so vividly was when the monetary aggregates were moving in opposite directions. Following the adoption of a Directive with some general prescription about the overall course of the aggregates, a Committee member with monetarist leanings said at the conclusion of the meeting, "But Alan, the aggregates are moving in opposite directions—how are you going to weight them?" Without a moment's hesitation Alan responded, "Oh, equally," and the meeting adjourned.

Notes

1. *U.S. Monetary Policy and Financial Markets* by Ann-Marie Meulendyke (New York: Federal Reserve Bank of New York, 1990), page 107.
2. Table provided by Ann-Marie Meulendyke for a lecture at Vanderbilt University.

Part IV

International Monetary Issues

12

Stephen H. Axilrod

The Globalization of
World Financial Markets

With good reason, the term "globalization" became a buzzword in the 1980s. The financial world is increasingly an internationally integrated one.

Globalization has a number of implications for businesses and public policy, including a key policy question about the extent to which countries' abilities to have independent economic policies have been eroded. With respect to monetary policies, for example, before the 1990s the discussion of policy independence usually referred to the domestic political independence of central banks. In the 1990s the independence discussion will refer more and more to whether globalized markets are limiting the economic independence of nations and central banks.

The proximate cause of globalization has been the elimination of exchange and capital controls that has occurred since the 1970s. The elimination of those controls is necessary, but not sufficient, for interdependence. People in one country must also be motivated to take advantage of opportunities in other countries, and must have the physical opportunity to do so. Both the motivation and the opportunities burgeoned in the 1980s and will develop further in the 1990s, which accounts for increasing globalization.

Besides deregulation and changing laws, two events have increased the amount of interdependence. One is quantitative—the emergence of Japan in the global market; and the other is qualitative—the emergence of a new financial technology.

The Emergence of Japan on the Financial Scene

While changing conditions within Japan pushed it to emerge as a force in global markets in the 1980s, Japan did not emerge on its own. Its emergence was partly related to the pull exerted by U.S. policy. There was both push and pull.

To get a full understanding of Japan's emergence, take yourself back to the beginning of the 1980s. At that time, Japan had a huge fiscal deficit. The United States was just beginning its major deficit period. In the early part of the 1980s, the U.S. fiscal stance began to change sharply as the huge tax cuts of 1982 were accompanied by an expansion in defense spending. Moreover, the shift toward fiscal expansion was accompanied by a large unexpected drop in the personal saving rate.

Many in the United States who favored those tax cuts thought that they would be financed by an increase in saving, but instead the United States experienced a consumer spending boom. The combined result of fiscal and consumer actions was a growing shortage of domestic saving in the United States relative to demand.

As the U.S. fiscal deficit was rising, Japan decided to lower its own fiscal deficit. Looking ahead, authorities there saw that the future tax rate necessary to finance the potential deficits, if policy did not change, was going to become intolerable. Japan was expecting its savings rate to decline and social security payments to rise over time with the aging of its population. So the Japanese made a policy decision to lower their fiscal deficit—as did many of the European countries at about the same time.

Once Japan decided to reduce its fiscal deficit while its savings rate remained relatively high, there was a clear potential for ex ante domestic saving to exceed ex ante domestic investment. The threatened result would be a collapse in the economy equalizing ex post domestic saving and investment at high levels of unemployment. Japan did not want that to happen. Its solution was to encourage the export industry. The resulting trade surplus provided an outlet abroad for the excess domestic saving.

The shift toward a trade-driven economic expansion was deliberate, but I do not believe Japan contemplated so large a shift in its trade position as developed. And so large a shift probably would not have occurred without the pull of the emerging U.S. domestic savings shortage. In any event, the push and pull together required a major integration of Japan's economy into the world economy.

The movement of Japanese saving abroad was welcomed by the United States as a means of financing its large fiscal deficit, or, to put it more generally, as a way of financing the excess of domestic investment over domestic saving. Without the inflow of Japanese saving, U.S. interest rates in the 1980s would have been even higher than they were, and the 1990 U.S. recession might have come sooner.

Let us now consider the results of Japan's emergence in terms of actual international flows of funds. In the 1975 to 1979 period, the major industrial countries experienced net capital outflows from residents of only $17.5 billion on average per year. That rose to $269 billion in 1989. So there has been an enormous increase in net long-term capital outflows from the industrial countries. No less than 25 percent of the rise came from Japan, as that country emerged onto the world financial stage.

The Japanese outflows reflected the activities of such institutions as trust banks, pension funds, and insurance companies, who increased their investments in foreign assets over the 1980s from a minimal amount to a range of 15 to 20 percent of their total securities assets. This represented a one-time adjustment by major Japanese institutions to a new situation. It was the dominant factor internationalizing the markets in the 1980s.

In the future, net long-term capital outflows from Japan will be much more moderate. They will be more in line with normal growth of institutional portfolios, rather than being stimulated by a restructuring of portfolios.

Nonetheless, even when net capital flows moderate in size, total gross cross-border flows will remain very large as markets remain closely linked. That is, once the Japanese become accustomed to dealing with foreign markets, and foreign markets become accustomed to dealing with Japan, there will continue to be a very large flow of funds between them—reflecting the buying and selling that accompanies speculative position taking, hedging operations, and other efforts to maximize returns.

To give you a sense of dimension, if I just look at net purchases of foreign public and corporate bonds, mainly public, by Japanese investors, they rose from $27 billion in 1984 to $94 billion in 1989—that is the net. But the gross transactions, the purchases and sales together, rose from $86 billion in 1984 to $3.3 trillion in 1989. So you can see that while the net increased, the gross increased by magnitudes more—close to fifty times more.

In 1990 and 1991 there was a sharp drop in the net capital outflows.

However, the gross flows declined only a little bit. So we have markets that have become very interrelated in good part because of the internationalization of the Japanese investor, who had not really been in the market before.

The Emergence of New Financial Technology

Japan's emergence as a major international player is a quantitative, not a qualitative, change for world markets. But almost at the same time, two qualitative changes did take place.

The first involves the speed of information flows. If you go to the Tokyo office of Nikko (the securities firm for which I work), you will see exactly the same trading screen as you would in the United States, not only at Nikko's U.S. office but in the trading rooms of major American firms. You can push the same buttons, and get the same information, as I can today at my desk in New York.

What this means, of course, is that people are beginning to be affected by the same gossip—some of it is fact, some of it is not; but it is there. They begin to see how prices are moving in New York and what affects them, and they get the same itchy feeling in Japan and New York.

The result of this technological change is an emerging common international culture among market participants. This is occurring even though the basic Japanese culture is radically different from the U.S. culture, even though Japanese business practices are radically different from U.S. business practices, and even though Japanese management is radically different from U.S. management.

Despite these differences, the traders in both countries are becoming very similar. Since traders are risk-takers with thin capital positions who necessarily act quickly, the response to the same flow of information is becoming more volatile as the number of traders and size of positions increases. That volatility can have adverse effects on the U.S. and world economy under certain circumstances—particularly if it happens to coincide with events that for a while exaggerate the volatility in one direction (the stock market crashes of 1987, for instance).

The second technological change is the emergence of derivatives and their related very sophisticated computer-based trading strategies. Most of these are hedging or arbitrage strategies. The latter are designed to take advantage of small departures in price relationships that somehow should not be there. Such arbitrage was always possible and was done when market differences were evident to the naked eye.

For finer distinctions with more complicated relationships, calculations by hand or with a calculator took an excessive length of time, and resources could not be effectively devoted to the effort. With modern computers, they take nanoseconds. This permits straddles, swaps, futures versus options strategies, and the like—all of ever-increasing amounts—which represent another major qualitative change. In today's financial markets the computer tells you when to push a button, and if you can push that button one second ahead of the other button-pusher, you may get in there and make some money.

The development of a common international trading culture and the ease and liquidity of trading through derivatives have contributed crucially to the enormous expansion in cross-border activity. Markets are becoming similar around the world, and ever more responsive one to the other, though there are and will remain differing degrees of response related to underlying economic differences among countries at particular times.

The impact of increasing financial globalization can be partially seen in the stock market crashes of October 1987, which were seminal events of the 1980s and signaled the beginning of the end of the speculative boom of the period and also highlighted some financial dangers in globalization.

The international interconnection of stock markets was carefully evaluated in an article on the stock market crash in the Federal Reserve Bank of New York's *Quarterly Review* for the summer of 1988. Let me stress four of its conclusions (found on pages 17, 38, and 45).

The first was that the spread of higher volatility from one major market to another was considerably greater in 1987 than the earlier statistical relationships would have predicted. That is just another way of saying, "Markets respond more promptly," which is what you would expect in this environment. When there is fear in the United States, the trader in Japan is going to wake up very scared. And if you wake up in London and you find people have been scared in Japan and the United States, you may get *very* scared.

A second conclusion was, "Viewed from a longer-term perspective, stock price movements in major markets have become increasingly similar in the 1980s, compared to the 1970s and before. This development generally consisted of the ongoing strengthening of cross-border trading, listing, and investment activities." The article did note, however, that the increased similarity of price movements over time was comparatively small. That allows, of course, for national differences in productivity growth and inflation to affect markets over the longer term.

A third conclusion was, "For the three largest equities markets [which would be New York, Tokyo, and London], a discernible role for cross-border investment and overseas trading in equities during the market break was confined to two instances, heavy sales by nonresidents in Tokyo on October 20 and price declines in UK ADR's [American Depository Receipts] in New York around October 19 [1987]."

Put another way, the observable international linkages through actual cross-border flows were unimportant. However, the mere fact that the actual net flows across borders were minor in the 1987 episode suggests that a major international contagion effect does exist. You can have a contagion effect across markets affecting domestic investors without an actual international flow, and this is much more likely in today's environment of instant communication and a more common market culture. You just scare the daylights out of the other side.

The final conclusion of the New York Fed's study that I would like to point to was indeed that "the principal international linkage between international stock markets appears to be an unobservable and indirect one created when sharp price declines in overseas markets contribute to market psychology." As we all have come to live in the same house, so to speak, contagion becomes more likely.

Interconnection with Macroeconomic Policies

Governmental reactions to the 1987 market crash illustrate how the process of globalization can affect the formulation of macroeconomic policies, in this case mainly monetary policies around the industrialized world.

The stock market declines had a very substantial effect on the psychology of central bankers, who had visions of the 1930s repeating themselves and were also well aware that one reason among others for the crashes of October 1987 was fear that international cooperation was breaking down. As a result, the immediate response to the stock market crashes—and the correct response, in my opinion—was to make sure that there was plenty of liquidity available through the major central banks. The only problem was that the policy was prolonged to the point where inflation accelerated.

In 1988 and 1989, the inflation rate in the United States was on the order of 5 percent, up from the 3.5 percent to 4 percent that the Fed had left us with following the 1981–82 recession. I am not criticizing the Fed; it *should* have been afraid that the stock market crash on a worldwide basis would lead to very bad economic conditions. In response it pushed money into the economy and dropped short-term interest rates, but the policy was not reversed soon enough once it became clear that real economic activity was holding up well. The inevitable result was more inflation.

At the time of the market crash, Germany and Japan had zero or negative inflation rates. In response to the crash, they also decided they could not afford the kind of tight policies that would keep inflation down to that level. In the end, their inflation rates began rising to a 3-3.5-percent range.

Thus, in response to stock market events, we got expansionary monetary policies around the industrial world. However, the central banks were not about to let that continue indefinitely. They eventually had to tighten.

The tightening that occurred in Japan in late 1989 and early 1990 led to a sustained and large stock market decline. Over the first three months of 1990, there was a drop in the Japanese market that was pretty much equivalent to the one-day drop the United States had in the crash of 1987.

These two crashes are related. The valuation of the Japanese market was relatively well sustained for two-and-a-half years or so after the U.S. crash, essentially through a monetary easing that went on for too long. Japanese inflation rose after 1987, but it remained relatively low—rising from zero to about 3 percent—and did not seem to have much impact on investor attitudes. In addition, domestic investors in Japan were not as truly internationalized as domestic investors in other countries at that time, so they responded less to the worldwide movement toward more realistic market valuations. But their highly adverse experience thus far in the 1990s has probably made Japanese equity investors realize that their domestic markets cannot be isolated from the rest of the world.

When the Bank of Japan was forced to tighten, and raised interest rates sharply, that led to a sharp downward revaluation in all assets. In particular, stock prices in Japan fell very sharply because they were furthest out of line with world values. Domestic investors there attempted to get hold of paper profits all at once, with the predictable result that the profits quickly disappeared and turned into large losses.

I think the Japanese market acted like the U.S. market but with a two-and-a-half-year lag. The crash of 1987 in the United States and the crash of 1990 in Japan signified the end of a huge speculative bubble around the world. In a globalized world, some major markets may for a while remain out of line with others, but they will eventually be brought into line as they respond to underlying factors, such as real capital costs, that are pervasive around the industrial world. Markets would be brought into line either from forced policy changes within a country that affect investor behavior or from international contagion effects or actual international flows.

Future Issues in Globalization

Let me conclude with a brief discussion of an important issue of globalization in the 1990s: the move in the EC toward a common currency. The move highlights issues of central bank independence in globalized markets. The common currency should be distinguished from the Common Market, which implies free trade in goods, services, capital, and labor, but not necessarily a common currency.

The idea of a common currency with a single central bank (with branches in the various countries) took root because the major countries in Europe recognized that, given their close interconnections, they could not in practice undertake economic policies that were for long independent of each other. I am assuming countries continue to eschew capital and exchange controls.

The countries have been planning to move toward a common currency by late this decade through a series of steps and after their economies have converged further. Until 1992, the various national currencies were linked through a set of fixed (within narrow limits) exchange rates in the ERM (Exchange Rate Mechanism). The ERM countries further agreed implicitly to give the policy lead to the country with the strongest economy and the soundest policy, which has been Germany. A set of fixed exchange rates necessarily limits the policy flexibility of all but one of the countries involved.

So the countries in effect hooked on to German monetary policy in order to keep inflation contained. That did not always have completely satisfactory effects, however. When Germany decided to tighten, all the countries had to tighten and raise interest rates so as to keep the exchange rates from moving outside the agreed bounds. The difficulty is that the required increase in interest rates sometimes may not be consistent with domestic economic conditions in a particular country. That led to the problems in the ERM, with a number of countries bailing out.

In any event, once you get to that point where you no longer have any independent monetary policy in the countries (except for Germany), the natural next step is to ask: "Why should we go through all this? Why don't we all just have a common currency?" A common currency would avoid the elaborate ERM mechanism and would eliminate any market doubts about the sustainability of exchange rate relationships set in the ERM. With a common currency, all the countries subsume themselves in the bigger whole, and there is no question of an independent monetary policy.

The political ramifications of such a change are substantial. As of now, no central bank in Europe, other than the German Bundesbank, is independent within its own political sphere—that is, none can make policy decisions independent of the executive branch of government. Moreover, as noted above, countries in the ERM, other than Germany, cannot implement an independent monetary policy on economic grounds since they have in practice tied themselves to German policy partly as a means of bringing about a convergence of their economies—a precondition for shifting to a common currency in the future.

A common currency and central bank as presently conceived by the Europeans would have two effects. First, the central bankers of all the countries would become independent of the executive branches of government by becoming part of the common central bank, which is planned to have independent status. Second, the dominance of Germany in European monetary policy would be diluted because it would be only one among a number of voting members on the central bank's board.

You can therefore see the strong appeal of the common central bank to the central bankers of France, the Netherlands, and other countries. European central bankers believe that they could come closer to achieving price stability if they were politically independent, and the central bankers outside Germany would also be able to have more of a policy input through a common central bank than when Germany is so dominant.

By the same token, a common currency and central bank may not look so attractive to Germany, which would in effect lose the degree of independence it now has by being subsumed in a greater whole. The natural result of these political realities is that Germany, as I interpret it, has been dragging its heels to some extent in moving toward the common currency. It has been doing so by insisting on tough conditions for convergence of economies and of fiscal policies that do not appear realistic at the moment for a number of countries, such as the U.K., Italy, or Spain, all of which withdrew from the ERM in 1992.

In the final analysis, the drive toward a single currency bloc will be determined by politicians, not by central bank technicians. It will come about—if it does—as part of the continuing effort within Europe to defuse centuries-old political tensions among the countries. A common currency in that context would help to broaden identity from the nation-state toward Europe as a whole, though additional political tensions may well arise if reduced identity of the nation-state also entails more localized demands for self-government.

If one assumes that Western Europe will eventually—despite the difficulties—become a unified currency bloc, the question naturally arises about relationships between that bloc and the United States and Japan. Obviously, Europe gets more weight as a unit in world financial flows and markets. We will then have three very large financial blocs in the world with, in my view, an even greater capacity than now for large international capital flows. The reason for this is that a unified Europe will be a much more liquid and open market than the individual country markets now are. As a result they will be much more exposed to large international flows—both in and out—than even now.

Sometimes capital flows in a globalized market are stabilizing—for example, when they willingly move toward areas with current account deficits and provide time for authorities to make needed domestic adjustments in an orderly way. At other times, however, they may be destabilizing—when confidence is lost in an area's overall policies, for instance—and force rapid or extreme domestic adjustments.

A none too startling conclusion is that continued progress toward greater globalization is an argument for more international economic cooperation—in order to keep problems in one large country or market from being communicated to others. This may become even more urgent when there are three large currency blocs with greater capacity to harm or help each other than when there are a large number of smaller currencies that do not individually carry as much weight and whose markets are not large or liquid enough to attract international funds.

13

SCOTT E. PARDEE

A Trader's View of the Foreign Exchange Market

The foreign exchange market spans the globe, with trading virtually around the clock. The amounts of money exchanged are huge, with close to $1 trillion a day changing hands. It has no central marketplace, and yet it is linked together by modern communications equipment—telephones, telexes, faxes, and computers. At any point in time there may be some 10,000 people around the world at their telephones, at their computer terminals, or in trading pits ready to buy or sell in response to the flow of political events, economic data, and rumors that affect their expectations. The pace is hectic.

Foreign exchange is a collection of international markets in time as well as space. If you want to be paid for goods to be delivered three months from now, or even five years from now, you can arrange to enter into a forward exchange contract with a bank, at a separate exchange rate for that date of delivery in the future, as distinct from a cash trade when the goods are delivered. If you want to invest in D-marks for three months, you can arrange a swap, buying spot marks and selling forward marks, which effectively eliminates your exchange risk. If you wish to speculate, you can trade futures on organized exchanges such as the Chicago Mercantile Exchange, based on the open-cry system developed in the U.S. commodity markets. The gamut of options trades (puts and calls) is also available through the banks and through the organized exchanges. Computers assist at every stage of a transaction—from analyzing a trading strategy to clearing the funds after a trade is done.

The Major Players

Banks are at the center of the foreign exchange market. They clear the dollars, the British pounds, the German marks, and the Japanese yen that change hands internationally. For the world's largest banks, foreign exchange is a major service to customers and, in most years, banks make substantial profits in trading for their own accounts.

Securities companies, independently or linked to banks, have also become major providers of foreign exchange services to their customers, drawing on their global office networks. Much of their business is linked to securities underwriting and trading, in cross-border or cross-currency transactions. But securities companies also seek to profit from trading for their own accounts.

As providers of foreign exchange services to customers, both banks and securities houses offer a wide array of highly specialized transactions, called derivative products, using futures and options strategies. The competition is fierce, both in pricing existing types of transactions and in developing new products.

Companies are important participants in the exchange markets, ranging from the one-product exporter or importer to the multinational giant. Some major companies, such as IBM, effectively have their own international balance of payments, engaging in exports and imports, direct investments, portfolio investments, and cash management activities. The corporate treasurer, who must manage the company's overall currency exposure in possibly dozens of currencies, may oversee a trading room as large and complex as those found in the banks and securities firms. As a rule, U.S. companies seek to hedge their exposures rather than to engage in outright speculation. But even that is a difficult job.

Portfolio investors, such as insurance companies, pension funds, and mutual funds, have turned increasingly to international capital and money markets, and are now a major force in the exchange market. At times, they are the dominant force, in view of the magnitude of funds they deal in. For example, Japanese investors hold close to $400 billion equivalent of foreign stocks and bonds. Whenever they become nervous about the dollar, they have two choices, to sell the securities and repatriate their funds, or to leave their investments alone but sell dollars forward in the exchange market to hedge the currency risk. Such transactions can be in the billions of dollars on a given day.

There is also a class of traders who trade currencies for profit, using their own money or managing the risk positions for others. Some of these traders are intraday or day-to-day players who chop small profits out of small positions, and in the process add liquidity to the market.

But others build sizable positions over time and can have an effect on the overall market when they suddenly rush to take their profits on those positions (or losses, as the case may be).

Finally, of course, there are the central banks. Market participants have to understand fully the exchange rate policies of the countries whose currencies they deal in. In some cases, the exchange rates are pegged, as under the rules of the European Community's Exchange Rate Mechanism. The central banks intervene in the market within prescribed limits. This allows little scope for day-to-day movement, say between the D-mark and the French franc, but does set up possibilities of large profits if the German and French governments should decide to change the central rate between their currencies, which happens infrequently. The dollar is floating against other major currencies, but the Federal Reserve and other central banks occasionally intervene when the market becomes especially disorderly or when the dollar rises or falls too far too fast for comfort.

With so many participants in the exchange market, all poised to move quickly, new events may lead to sudden surges in trading. Indeed, exchange rates may even move abruptly for no apparent reason at all. My rule of thumb is to try to guess why traders are doing what they are doing. The exchange rate may seem to be moving irrationally, but the market participants all have solid reasons why they, individually, are buying or selling.

Influences on the Foreign Exchange Market

Trade flows—exports, imports—are a major influence on foreign exchange markets. However, exchange rates do not move lock-step with the movement of goods. Exporters and importers rely on futures and forward markets and on credit facilities to convert funds from one currency to another at the most advantageous price. If you are exporting to Germany and you expect the Deutsche mark to rise relative to the dollar, you will wait until the last minute to convert your mark proceeds so that you can take advantage of the appreciation of the mark in the meantime. If you are an importer, however, you will hurry to convert your dollars into marks right away lest a delay force you to pay more dollars later on. Such leads and lags can be a major force influencing the exchange market, and frequently depend on swings in market psychology.

I can take you through every item of the balance of payments to explain how the flows of funds affect the market. And in each case, I would point out how market participants lead and lag their transactions in response to shifting expectations toward exchange rate movements. Interest rates are another major factor influencing exchange rates. If short-term interest rates are at 8 percent in Germany and at 5 percent in the United States, why would anyone keep liquid funds in the United States when you can earn 3 percent per annum overnight in Germany? When people see such discrepancies, they gravitate toward the higher interest rate market as long as they have confidence that the currency will not decline for other reasons. In quiet times, large amounts of money do move in response to such differentials as corporate treasurers, portfolio managers, and money managers seek to maximize their current interest yields (or minimize their current interest costs).

But not all short-term money is interest sensitive—there is also "hot money." Political and economic uncertainties can scare market participants to move from one currency to another. The German mark these days is heavily influenced by events in Eastern Europe and the former Soviet Union. Greater uncertainty on Germany's eastern borders frequently prompts selling pressures on the D-mark. A relaxation of tensions may lead to a rally for the D-mark. The dollar is frequently considered a safe haven in times of crisis.

With 10,000 people all poised to buy or sell, the individual trader has to develop knee-jerk responses to certain types of events that are likely to move the market suddenly. If you do not respond quickly, you may be too late. Indeed, the trick is to act before the event hits the market and others begin to respond.

The market does not always respond in the same way to the same kind of event. I grew up when the United States had lots of oil, and Europe and Japan were considered energy deficient. In 1973, when the first oil crisis hit, the traders' knee-jerk reaction was to buy dollars on the view that a higher oil price would help the United States and hurt Europe and Japan. But now, in the 1990s, we import more than half of the oil we consume, and Europe and Japan have become much more energy efficient. When Saddam Hussein invaded Kuwait and the oil price spiraled to $40 a barrel in August 1990, today's generation of traders sold dollars on the view that the United States would suffer more than Europe and Japan. To avoid being out of step, foreign exchange traders spend a lot of time talking to each other, swapping scenarios to learn how other traders, and the market generally, might react to upcoming events. Traders must continuously reprogram themselves so that their knee-jerk reactions are in the right direction.

Supply and demand curves from the foreign exchange market are different from the textbook models. Normally, if a price rises, one would expect the quantity demanded to decline and the quantity supplied to increase, leading to a falling back of the price to a stable equilibrium level. But in the exchange market, there are frequently times when market sentiment is heavily weighted in favor of one currency such that the rise in price triggers massive new demands and a drying up of supply as traders jump on the bandwagon—that is, equilibria are often unstable. Such explosive volatility can lead to serious overshooting of exchange rates to levels that are politically or economically intolerable, and is the prime justification for central bank intervention, even in a floating exchange rate system.

Trading Strategies of Market Participants

While every generation of foreign exchange traders comes up with new terminology, they all rely on three basic strategies. The first is to trade on economic fundamentals, comparing GDP, exports, imports, relative rates of inflation, and money supply growth of different countries. A country that has strong economic growth, a large trade surplus, low inflation, and good control over the growth of money and credit aggregates will have a strong currency. The United States has not done well in many of these categories in recent years, experiencing slow economic growth, a large and persistent current account deficit, a high rate of inflation relative to our major trading partners, and uncontrollable credit demands (especially by the federal government) that force us to be dependent on foreign capital to help finance both our fiscal deficit and the current account deficit. These factors lead to a persistent weakness of the dollar against other currencies. A whole generation of foreign exchange traders has learned to expect that the dollar will continue to decline as long as these conditions continue. Thus, in their knee-jerk reactions, they are quicker to sell dollars on bad news than to buy dollars on good news. This was not always the case—we used to say, "Buy dollars and wear diamonds."

The second strategy relies on charting and technical analysis of price behavior. Traders follow exchange rate movements closely to identify patterns of repetitive behavior. If you find a price pattern developing that looks promising for the dollar, irrespective of other information available to you, you buy dollars. If the price pattern changes, you change your position. Traders routinely compare notes on the relative "support points" below the current exchange rate, at which previous price behavior suggests buying will emerge, and "resistance points" above the current exchange rate, at which past behavior suggests that selling will emerge. In the search for predictable patterns, traders have increasingly resorted to high-speed computers and sophisticated mathematical models.

Indeed, people who are skilled in these techniques offer their services to clients. Such models are often referred to as "black boxes," since the people who develop the models consider their techniques of analysis to be proprietary secrets and only tell customers when the models give a buy or sell signal. I am especially wary of the black box approach. Foreign exchange is a zero-sum game. Even with 50–50 odds, if ten people start with black box approaches, five will have profits in the first year, two or three of those will have profits in the second year, and one or two will still have profits in the third year. This is why sophisticated investors insist on seeing a five-year track record before buying into a black box service. And even then, events unforeseen by the black boxes may cause devastating losses.

The third trading strategy is an omnibus approach: look at everything, not just at economic fundamentals or past price behavior. Political forces are important. And by this, I do not refer only to wars, revolutions, and other cataclysmic events that cause hot money flows. On a day-to-day basis, public officials may make comments that have profound effects on exchange rates. In 1991, then–Treasury Secretary Brady was quoted as forecasting a third quarter GDP growth rate of 2 percent, more than expected. Traders bought dollars on the view that the stronger GDP growth would lead to a rise in U.S. interest rates. Later in the day, Federal Reserve Chairman Alan Greenspan was quoted as saying that the "economy is still soft." Traders quickly sold dollars, on the expectation that the Fed might ease monetary policy and interest rates might fall.

In a global market, comments by public officials can lead to considerable confusion among traders. I remember an occasion in the late 1970s when Germany's Chancellor Helmut Schmidt was quoted by the wire services as saying that he favored an appreciation of the D-mark, a comment that led to heavy buying of D-marks in the exchange market. Later that day, a spokesman for the German government went on TV and denied that Chancellor Schmidt had said such a thing. When American traders read the denial on their news tickers, they sold D-marks on the expectation that the rest of the market would take denial at face value. But they were shocked to find German traders still buying marks. The Germans had seen the spokesman on TV. He was smiling so broadly that they saw that he did not believe what he was saying! Nowadays, trading rooms are all equipped with cable TV.

Some Practical Considerations

In the early 1990s, I advised customers in Japan and elsewhere in Asia to buy German government bonds rather than U.S. bonds. The reasoning is based on different national attitudes toward inflation, and the current levels of interest rates. In the United States, a moderate amount of inflation is tolerated—3 percent to 4 percent per annum—and this is reflected in U.S. economic policy. If inflation here reaches 6 percent or higher, then public pressure builds up on the government to reduce it. By contrast, in Germany, where many families have suffered ruinous inflation in their lifetimes, 1 percent is as much as the public tolerates, and a 2 percent rate causes real concern. In 1992, because of the costs of unification of East and West Germany, the inflation rate surged to 4 percent per annum, and the ten-year government bond rose in yield to 8 percent. It is a safe bet that Germany, through tight money policy of the Bundesbank, will reduce its inflation rate back to 2 percent or less, which means that German bond yields will drop to 5 percent or less. In the United States, bond yields in 1992 were at 8 percent, well above the inflation rate of 4 percent. The United States is not so likely to reduce inflation to 2 percent or lower, and the best one can hope for is a reduction of a bond yield to 6 percent or so. The spread in short-term rates was even wider. Not only will investors place their money in Germany over the United States, but foreign exchange traders will buy and hold D-marks on the expectation that Germany will receive heavy capital inflows.

Foreign exchange traders basically prefer volatile markets to stable ones, especially markets that move prices in a predictable way; that is the source of the adage, "the trend is your friend." But traders are not always objective about the direction of the trend. My best example is in the stock market. Your broker recommends a stock, you study it, and you make a careful decision to buy. If the price goes up, you were right, and are satisfied with your own good judgment. But if the stock goes down, then someone else is wrong—your broker who sold you a bill of goods, the people who are so foolish as to be selling the stock, or even the rascals who are rigging the market against you. There ought to be a law! The crash on October 19, 1987, was terrible for many investors, whose portfolios lost 25 percent to 30 percent of their value overnight, and led to a political outcry.

In any financial market, when there are large losses to traders and investors, pressure builds up on the authorities to stop price movement. Foreign exchange rates are a double-edged sword. If the dollar rises or falls too far, someone is badly hurt and calls for action to halt the movement or reverse it. Even in a floating exchange rate regime, such as the dollar is under now, when there are periods of extensive volatility, the traders will be the first to call for intervention to stabilize the markets.

Indeed, market participants must be ever alert to the possibility that a sudden forceful intervention by major central banks will halt or reverse a trend in exchange rates, causing huge losses to the individuals who bet that they would not intervene, or that if they did, they would not succeed. During such times there is a lot of macho talk in the market, especially when the central bank intervention appears timid, but seasoned traders remember the times the central banks were successful, and are wary. The government cannot allow exchange rates to get so far out of line that domestic economies are affected adversely, and sooner or later the central banks will win.

Finally, a trader has to choose between active versus passive approaches to trading. There are many academic papers showing that most stock pickers would have done better if they had chosen stocks randomly, or by throwing darts at a dart board. There are a few exceptions, such as the magnificent performance of the Magellan Fund up until 1992. Very few people succeed with an active approach to trading. But traders who follow a passive approach also court disaster. If you trade to beat an index and the index is going down, you are still losing money. In such a case, you would be better to be out of the market altogether. That is why many traders now talk in terms of a risk–reward ratio. If the risk is too great, better to stand aside and watch, even though you may be missing a profit opportunity.

Being a trader is an exciting life. Sometimes it is lucrative, and individuals become millionaires. But many others fall by the wayside. You never know how good you are until you actually get involved. Let me close with a few lines from a book that almost every trader in Wall Street reads, *Reminiscences of a Stock Operator*, written back in the 1920s by a plunger.

> I have heard of people who amuse themselves conducting imaginary operations in the stock market to prove with imaginary dollars how right they are. Sometimes these ghost gamblers make millions. It is very easy to be a plunger that way. It is like the old story of the man who was going to fight a duel the next day. His second asked him, "Are you a good shot?" "Well," said the dueler, "I can snap the stem of a wine-glass at 20 paces." "That's all very well," said the unimpressed second, "but can you snap the stem of a wine-glass while the wine-glass is pointing a loaded pistol straight at your heart?"[1]

Things are a little different in the real world than they are in theory, and anyone who is trying to understand international monetary issues must understand both.

Note

1. Edwin Lefevre, *Reminiscences of a Stock Operator*, originally published in 1923 by George H. Dorman Co., New York, and republished in 1980 by Books of Wall Street, Frances Management Association, Burlington, Vermont.

14

MARGARET GREENE

Monetary and Exchange Rate Policy Implementation

In June 1975, Alan Holmes was asked to take on, in addition to his domestic responsibilities, senior responsibility for the Foreign Function. This is the part of the Bank that conducts operations in foreign currencies for the U.S. Treasury and the Federal Reserve and also provides correspondent banking services in the United States for other central banks and international monetary institutions.

At the time that Alan Holmes was given the dual assignment for the domestic and foreign "desks" at the Federal Reserve, many wondered whether the creation of the dual assignment had policy significance. In the United States, monetary policy and exchange rate policy were traditionally believed to have different goals and rely on different tools. But already in 1975 there was an acute sense that the world was changing and policy administration might have to adjust in response. The United States was just emerging from two episodes that drew particular attention to the growing exposure of our domestic economy and banking system to developments abroad:

1. The first oil crisis of the early 1970s, in which oil prices rose fourfold, patterns of international trade and capital flows were changed abruptly, and oil exporting countries amassed what then seemed to be huge amounts of funds to be recycled in the world's money and capital markets.

   There had hardly been a time in the postwar period when the United States appeared to be so much at the mercy of forces beyond its control. And never before had markets had to absorb such large amounts of funds, held and controlled by so few, deposited in such a small number of institutions, and placed (at least initially) in so narrow a range of financial instruments.

2. The closure of a small bank in Germany, which, because it had large outstanding payments arising from its foreign exchange operations on the day it was closed, threatened to have severe consequences for payments and settlements in dollars for banks here in the United States and around the world.

This bank had developed a reputation for taking extremely large positions in foreign exchange, so many were not surprised that the banking supervisory authorities in Germany would, in time, find losses in its foreign exchange positions to be of a size to warrant closing the bank. What had not been appreciated beforehand was that, even though the German authorities had taken care to wait to close the bank until after the close of business in Europe, the U.S. banking system could still be so disrupted. When banks that had routinely made payments to this bank in marks during the German business day discovered that they would not be receiving the countervalue in dollars the same day in New York because, by that time, the bank had been officially closed, near-panic ensued. No event before or since has so dramatically demonstrated the settlement risk inherent in foreign exchange trading; some people still refer to settlement risk as "Herstatt" risk, after the name of the bank involved.

Since 1975, the interdependencies of the world economy and the linkages of developments abroad to those here at home have become even more apparent. Official barriers to international financial flows have been nearly eliminated, especially in the last decade. Other institutional barriers have also been reduced, so that the role of nationality in determining access to key domestic financial markets has declined substantially. With the move to floating exchange rates, the transmission mechanisms by which economic or financial impulses from one country are felt in others has also been altered. Thus, both the economic and financial environment in which monetary policy decisions are made has changed—sometimes more quickly or to a greater extent than policymakers at the time realized. This observation leads us to question whether the relationship between monetary and exchange rate policy has changed, and if so, how.

The Theoretical Linkages Between
Monetary and Exchange Rate Policy

The linkages between monetary and exchange rate policy are extremely interesting and complex, and space does not allow adequate coverage of this issue here. For the purpose of this essay, the substantive issue is the extent that monetary and exchange rate policies can be or are independent of each other.

That there are important linkages is clear. Consider that:

- The domestic interest rate is a price that relates the value of domestic currency in the future to the value of domestic currency today.

- The spot exchange rate is a price that relates the value of domestic currency today to the value of a foreign currency today.

- The forward exchange rate (that is, the price you agree today to pay to exchange domestic currency for foreign currency in, say, three months' time) is the price that relates the value of a foreign currency to the value of domestic currency over time.

Monetary policy operates on the availability and the cost of money and credit in the economy and as such has a bearing on the supply of domestic currency, relative to foreign currency, as well as on interest rates.

Exchange rate policy operates on the terms under which domestic currency can be exchanged for foreign currency and therefore has a bearing on exchange rates, spot and forward.

The ultimate goals of monetary policy are usually domestic—such as price stability, full employment, and sustainable economic growth. The question we want to focus on is whether recent experience suggests that these domestic objectives need to take account of a country's exchange rate or balance of payments position. Or do we need to go even further? There is an increasing trend to try to make macroeconomic policy goals consistent across countries, giving rise to what is known as the "coordination" process.

The ultimate goals of exchange rate policy are usually international—sustainable balance of payments position, acceptable exchange rate level or trend, and adequacy of a country's international reserve position. The question is, does recent experience suggest that these international objectives need to be consistent with domestic conditions and underlying economic realities so that, for example, monetary policy or a central bank's interest rate actions may have to be adjusted to meet an exchange rate or official reserves goal?

In examining these questions, it is interesting to note that while central banks have many monetary policy tools they can use to seek to attain their policy objectives, they are increasingly relying on techniques that effect changes in the supply of reserves in the banking system. Those engaging in open market operations for monetary policy purposes focus on the quantity of reserves to be supplied or absorbed, taking into account targets for monetary growth, if they have been established, or money market conditions, to the extent they are considered to reflect demand and supply for reserves. Otherwise, market forces determine short-term interest rates.

Although central banks have several exchange rate policy tools they can use, a principal instrument of exchange rate policy is intervention. Intervention is an open market operation in the exchange market that occurs when a central bank buys or sells foreign exchange for the purpose of affecting the foreign exchange value of its own currency. Those engaging in foreign exchange market operations tend not to have as an objective the quantity of currency to be bought or sold. Rather, they focus on obtaining a desired impact on current market conditions or prices and adjust the size of the operation to try to achieve the intended result—within limits, of course. They may try to take advantage of psychological or other transitory factors to accomplish their immediate objectives most efficiently.

The linkages between the implementation of these two policies arise from the impact of these operations on variables other than the target variables of the operation. On the one side, a change in monetary policy that prompts the market to make an adjustment in short-term interest rates may, because of the current abundant supply of internationally mobile capital, generate such large flows of funds from one country to another as to have a material impact on the exchange rate. This situation has given rise to a debate over the extent that monetary policy operates through interest rates and the demand and supply of credit, as conventionally thought, or through changes in the exchange rate that influence price and output levels in different sectors of the real economy. On the other side, a foreign exchange market operation can supply or absorb reserves of the banking system because when a central bank buys the exchange it is selling its own currency or, alternatively, when it sells the exchange it is buying its own currency. As a result there are many people who question the extent to which exchange rate policy—at least as it relates to intervention operations of the central bank—is distinguishable from monetary policy.

In an effort to distinguish exchange rate policy from monetary policy, at least for analytical purposes, economists refer to intervention as being either "nonsterilized" or "sterilized."

In nonsterilized intervention, the foreign exchange operation is permitted to have an effect on banks' reserves. A central bank that purchases foreign exchange for domestic currency pays the banks for the currency it bought by crediting the banks' reserve accounts at the central bank and, as a result, the reserves of the banking system increase.

In sterilized intervention, the impact of the foreign exchange operation is completely offset by the central bank. After the central bank credits banks' reserves for its purchase of foreign exchange, it then turns around and sells domestic securities from its portfolio to the banks to absorb the reserve effect of the intervention. In effect, the central bank ends up reducing its holdings of domestic bonds and increasing its holdings of foreign currency, which it may then invest in foreigncurrency denominated bonds.

Central banks differ in the extent that they can, or choose to, sterilize their foreign exchange market intervention as a matter of day-to-day practice. For the United States, the size of a day's foreign exchange market interventions is small relative to the size of the domestic money market and the Federal Reserve's holdings of securities. Therefore, the Federal Reserve has not experienced any constraints in sterilizing its foreign currency operations. But many other central banks may be less likely to conduct their intervention operations on a sterilized basis as a matter of daily routine, even if they try to sterilize their intervention operations in full or in part over time. For some countries foreign exchange interventions are so large relative to the size of the domestic money market and the central bank's holdings of domestic securities that they even use foreign exchange operations as an important or principal tool of domestic monetary policy implementation, usually on an unsterilized basis.

Central banks differ, also, in the extent that they have responsibility for monetary and/or exchange rate policy. In almost every case the central bank executes all open market operations in both domestic and exchange markets. Differences arise in the extent that individual decisions of the central bank need to be ratified by the executive branch (in a presidential form of government) or by the cabinet (in a parliamentary form of government).

In the United States, Federal Reserve decisions do not have to be ratified by the president or one of his appointees in the executive branch. The Federal Reserve is the only institution charged with monetary policy responsibilities. It has also taken on some responsibilities for foreign currency operations at the request of the U.S. Treasury—and holds some of the U.S. foreign currency reserves—there being a distinct advantage to having an institution like the Federal Reserve that can work in cooperation with foreign central banks and can enter into transactions with market participants on professional terms. But it is the secretary of the Treasury, as representative of the president, who is responsible for the international or foreign financial policies of the United States. He has political accountability for any commitments or understandings that the United States undertakes with other nations or international institutions, and that provide the general framework for U.S. intervention operations in the exchange market. The Federal Reserve and the Treasury each report to the Congress, and thereby to the people as a whole, on their respective operations and areas of competence. The current arrangements imply that there must be considerable day-to-day consultation and decision making when it comes to exchange rate policy.

In other countries, the role of the central bank and its relation to the finance ministry varies considerably. In a few, the central bank is independent both with respect to monetary and exchange rate policy, and the central bank holds the country's official reserves in its own name. In some cases the central bank has greater autonomy in matters relating to monetary policy than in those relating to exchange rate policy; the central bank may hold reserves for the government and execute exchange rate operations in accordance with government, or finance ministry, directives. In some cases, the central bank works closely with the finance ministry, which is publicly accountable for both monetary and exchange rate matters.

Whatever the institutional framework, the extent to which a central bank can assert itself in the policy debate depends on the quality and reputation of the central bank, the persuasiveness of its arguments, and the forcefulness of its leadership. The fact that the central bank does have operational responsibility provides it with both a unique expertise—in terms of implementation and tactics—and a unique asset—market intelligence.

Linkages Between Monetary and Exchange Rate Policy in Practice

The floating of exchange rates ushered in a new environment for monetary/exchange rate policy decision making. Central banks were relieved of the responsibility for maintaining the value of their currency within specified and narrow ranges around fixed parities. Under these circumstances, many economists believed that monetary policy would not have to be subordinated to international objectives but, for the first time in the postwar period, would be allowed to be directed unambiguously toward domestic objectives. In the first blush of enthusiasm of the floating rate period, it was widely thought that each country could establish its own policy priorities, leaving movements in the exchange rate to adjust to whatever inflation differentials developed. It was assumed these exchange rate adjustments would proceed relatively smoothly.

The United States Learns About Interdependence

Such was the approach the United States took in the late 1970s. The Carter administration promised high employment, the containment of inflation, reduced dependence on imported energy, and tax reduction, believing that the international environment gave the United States license—indeed, an obligation—to expand more rapidly than others. What followed was a series of exchange market disturbances that in effect reflected the impossibility of one country—even one with the economic size and importance of the United States—proceeding in a direction inconsistent with that elsewhere.

Let me describe how this worked. Policymakers of the time could not convince market participants of the consistency of their own objectives. Nor could they assuage market fears that the administration's strategy was inconsistent with, and could ultimately be undermined by, the emerging deficit in the U.S. balance of payments position that required financing.

The market's skepticism about the U.S. policy approach was reflected in a weakening of the dollar in the exchange markets. As pressures against the dollar intensified, administration officials expressed concern about the decline of the dollar but appeared reluctant to do anything to stop it out of fear of jeopardizing their domestic objectives. In that environment the pressures only got worse and the market dynamics moved in a destabilizing direction—aggravating the inflation and trade problems of the United States and at the same time intensifying the trade surpluses and adding anti-inflationary impulses on the trade-surplus, low-inflation countries of Germany and Japan. Confidence in the ability of the U.S. administration to steer the country out of its economic problems withered. The U.S. monetary authorities intervened in the exchange markets, at times very heavily, at least in part to suppress the evidence of the growing lack of confidence in the macroeconomic management of the U.S. economy and to protect the credibility of the administration.

As the United States rode out this collision course between domestic policy objectives and market realities, private sector financing disappeared and the United States became dependent on central bank financing. The financing took the form of having central banks of the other major countries either buy dollars in the exchange markets or lend currencies to the United States, which the U.S. monetary authorities then used to buy dollars in the exchange markets. As the financing requirements built up, our creditor central banks imposed increasingly onerous policy conditions on the United States.

Thus, in the end, the United States did bow to international considerations to adjust its domestic policy objectives away from job creation and toward price stabilization and energy conservation to reduce the trade deficit. What we will never know is whether the cost, as measured by the extent to which the United States had to pare back its objectives for growth, was any less than it would have been had policy adjustments been made earlier on. My guess is that the cost was greater. What subsequent developments unambiguously revealed is that the United States had to accept a sustained period of monetary restraint in the early 1980s to offset the excesses that were permitted during the late 1970s.

The experience of the late 1970s is often cited as evidence that sterilized intervention is ineffective because the pressures on the dollar exchange rate were not relieved until the United States convincingly changed its monetary policy course. This judgment is probably too harsh. Although there were episodes of success for intervention in the 1977–79 experience, for the period as a whole it was not given much of a chance. It was called upon to perform a task for which it was not designed.

The lessons of the late 1970s have left a strong impression and shed a different light on the workings of economies in a regime of floating exchange rates. We no longer think of countries embarked on their own independent policy courses. There is a greater acknowledgment of the interdependencies of the world economy. We learned then that a country cannot obtain its own objectives without taking into account the objectives being pursued by others and the others' responses to what we do here at home.

The United States Adjusts to an Interdependent World

In the aftermath of the late 1970s, government objectives for economic policies became less ambitious and more focused on eliminating inflation. Confidence had been shaken in the ability to control the economy with countercyclical fiscal policies and fine tuning of monetary policy. Indeed, fiscal policy lost all flexibility, leaving monetary policy as the only major tool for short-term stabilization. Meanwhile, monetary policy was set on a medium-term course designed to curb over time the growth of monetary aggregates. Foreign exchange market intervention was not used extensively at this time, at least not in the United States. There was a strong belief in the ability of market forces to have a constructive effect on the economy. As the dollar started first to recover and then to become quite strong, there was the feeling that the exchange rate developments were helping to reinforce the anti-inflationary stance of monetary policy. Any attempt to resist the exchange rate move risked being misinterpreted as indicating a willingness to compromise the anti-inflation goal.

By the mid-1980s, major progress had been achieved in getting better convergence of price performance among the major industrialized countries. Monetary policy, when dedicated to the objective of containing inflation, was proving its effectiveness. However, the impact of monetary policies was beginning to be seen as operating not only through interest rates, as was traditionally thought. It was seen, also, as working through the exchange rate. With the United States experiencing perhaps the greatest turnaround in its monetary policy stance between the late 1970s and the early 1980s, the dollar had risen to levels considered to be very high. Output growth had slowed, particularly in the manufacturing sector most vulnerable to competitive pressures from abroad. The U.S. trade position had greatly deteriorated, arousing protectionist sentiment and raising questions about the sustainability of the existing exchange rate relationships. Concern therefore developed that a serious misalignment of exchange rates had occurred even though U.S. price performance had stabilized impressively.

Beginning in late 1985, the U.S. administration under Treasury Secretary Baker moved to address exchange rate misalignment. The United States and other major countries agreed, in the Plaza Agreement of September 1985, to encourage the appreciation of other currencies against the dollar and then, at the Louvre in February 1987, to limit the extent of the dollar's decline when the move in exchange rates seemed to be getting excessive. These understandings included an expression of a desirable development for certain exchange rates, reinforced on occasion by an intervention commitment. But in no way were the commitments limited to exchange rates and intervention. Indeed, participating countries undertook to put in place a variety of fiscal and other measures to backstop their exchange rate objectives and announced their intentions in an official communiqué. There was a hope that the process of entering into such agreements would increase the chance that the major countries' policies would be consistent both internally and internationally. The fulfillment of these policy commitments would have a constructive influence on exchange market developments, building on the initial announcement effects of the understandings or of any intervention operations.

These arrangements have given rise to the practice of having periodic meetings of finance ministers and central bank governors of the Group of Seven Countries (the United States, Germany, Japan, the UK, France, Canada, and Italy) in which each country's policies are reviewed by the others according to agreed-upon criteria. In many instances, the direction for economic policy is agreed upon and individual countries announce policy initiatives they will pursue to support shared goals. Frequently, these meetings do produce agreement about the desirable course of the principal exchange rates. Yet seldom do the policy understandings that have been reached in this process include specific monetary policy commitments, out of respect for the independence of a country's monetary policy.

This situation has at times led to some question in markets about the relationship between monetary and exchange rate policies since the Louvre Accord. There have been times when the overall policy objectives have been consistent with the participating central banks' monetary policies then in place, so there has been no uncertainty about the relationship between the two. But there have also been situations in which market participants perceived there to be a policy conflict, or a potential one. On some of these occasions, the central banks have attempted to indicate to markets their commitment toward working together—even if economic conditions in their countries sometimes require them to act in different directions—by trying to do that which they feel they must do in a coordinated way. For example, they may make major policy announcements at about the same time, or they may take some other action, such as a visible act of intervention, to signal to markets that they are still working together.

In any case, it is growing increasingly apparent that, even among the three largest countries, there is a link in practice between monetary and exchange rate developments. The central banks have generally been able to work cooperatively so as to meet their own monetary policy objectives while still contributing to greater exchange rate stability between the dollar, on the one hand, and the German mark and Japanese yen, on the other hand. Intervention has also been used since the Louvre Accord, sometimes to support the dollar and sometimes to contain its rise. On two occasions—January 1988 and February 1991—relatively modest intervention operations to support the dollar were quickly followed by a substantial recovery of the dollar exchange rate, giving evidence to some that intervention might be, under the right circumstances, more effective than previously believed.

Some European Countries
Institutionalize Interdependence

Notwithstanding the evident gains in providing for more stable evolution of dollar exchange rates, a number of European countries tried to make Europe a zone for further exchange rate stability. Consistent with broader political objectives for enhanced cooperation among European states, during the early 1990s the members of the European Community began to embark on a major effort to find ways to create a single market in Europe and work toward eventual monetary union. By now, most participating countries have eliminated any remaining restrictions on cross-border capital flows.

In moving toward monetary union, the EC central banks have strengthened multinational surveillance among themselves. They have tried to establish a common framework for monitoring monetary policy and to agree on assessing the compatibility of monetary policies among the participating countries. In this process, broad agreement was reached that monetary policy in each country be directed to price stability and be relieved of other tasks better achieved by other policies. Monetary policies were considered to be compatible if there is a convergence of inflation among the participating countries and if the policies are contributing to the avoidance of major exchange rate pressures.

As this process has unfolded, a number of countries placed increasing emphasis on the exchange rate as a guide to monetary policy. In some cases the monetary authorities were mainly concerned about the effects of currency depreciation on changes in domestic inflation. Curbing a decline in the exchange rate was thereby seen as contributing to the domestic policy goal of containing inflation or preventing inflation from abroad from adding to inflationary pressures at home. In these instances, exchange rate and monetary policies were seen as complementary.

In other countries, the authorities appeared to believe that by making explicit exchange rate commitments, the credibility of monetary policy was enhanced. The argument goes that if the authorities firmly link their currency with that of another country that is a suitably stable partner, market participants and residents would believe that the risk of future inflation has been diminished, the risk premium in domestic interest rates would gradually disappear, and market interest rates would actually decline relative to that of the partner currency as inflationary expectations subside. In this way the exchange rate became an intermediate objective of monetary policy.

A number of countries adopted such an approach. The Belgian authorities announced that the Belgian franc would remain closely linked to the strongest currency within the EMS and interest rate policies would normally be geared to keeping the margin of fluctuation for the Belgian franc/Deutsche mark exchange rate narrower than permitted within that arrangement. Outside the EMS, Austria and, to a lesser extent, Switzerland used the exchange rate for their currency relative to the German mark as a guide for monetary policy. Norway, Sweden, and Finland fixed central rates for their currencies in terms of the ECU (European Currency Unit) as an anchor for monetary policy. The efforts of those countries to bring greater exchange rate stability to Europe were impressive. The extent to which these efforts can hold up under the challenge of German unification will be one of the most important issues these countries will face as time goes on.

Implications of the Linkages of Monetary and Exchange Rate Policies on the Internal Organization of Central Banks

Have these trends in the development of monetary and exchange rate policies led central banks to bring the two operations closer together organizationally? Will there be, tomorrow, more individuals in the central banks around the world with the responsibilities that Alan Holmes had at the Federal Reserve between 1975 and 1981?

A number of factors or developments are forcing central banks at least to consider, if not to implement, a growing degree of integration of the monetary and exchange rate policy areas of their organizations. To be sure, some of these considerations are policy related. Others are more administrative, reflecting desires to reduce costs, avoid duplication of processing systems, provide for more job rotation and cross-fertilization of ideas, and integrate different cultures within a single organization.

To the extent that exchange market instruments are used for the implementation of domestic policy goals, there can be real advantages to having close cooperation, if not integration, between the two operations. One of the Nordic central banks was the first to reorganize in such a way. An important element in its decision to make an organizational change was the fact that exchange market swaps are a principal means by which the central bank provides domestic currency to the money market. For a long time, these operations had been performed by a foreign exchange department that had diverse responsibilities. By implementing a functional reorganization, this central bank hoped to improve policy coordination, avoid areas of potential conflict, and integrate some operations previously performed by the old foreign exchange department into departments conducting research or supervisory functions.

There are other European central banks that are in the process of moving in a similar direction for largely similar reasons. In most of these cases, the countries have small domestic money markets relative to the size of their foreign exchange markets, exchange market products are used as a tool of domestic monetary policy implementation, and intervention in the exchange markets is either not sterilized or is only partially sterilized so that when it occurs, it has important if only temporary monetary policy considerations. To the extent that these countries have also undertaken exchange rate commitments or are using their exchange rate as a guide or intermediate target for monetary policy, the link between the two operations is even stronger. Moreover, a number of these institutions are positioning themselves for the eventual establishment of a European central bank that may ultimately carry out many of these operations for participating countries as a whole. In the interim, organizational changes that can economize on staff, back office costs, or other scarce resources are welcome.

For countries where the business requirements for coordination of the domestic and exchange market operations are less clear, there is either: (1) less of an effort to combine the two operations, or (2) where efforts are under way, the process of coordinating operational and analytical staffs between exchange market and domestic market products has proven to be time-consuming and difficult.

The Bank of England started pursuing a "middle-of-the-road" course in this respect even before the United Kingdom assumed the responsibility of keeping its currency within the exchange rate mechanism of the EMS. The Bank has a long tradition of open market operations in both domestic markets and foreign exchange, and the market in London for sterling-denominated assets is unquestionably capable of supporting the central bank's operations. The Bank did establish senior management positions several years ago with responsibility for both the domestic money market and foreign exchange operations. Later on, the Bank of England redesigned the trading room to combine the two operations in one place. A number of the managers have had experience in both operations. Nevertheless, there still are important cultural and business differences between the two operations.

Among the major industrialized countries outside the European context, there are fewer examples of efforts to bring the two operations together. It may be that, for these countries, the use of distinctly different instruments in distinctly different markets reduces the scope both for enhanced policy execution and coordination. The operational requirements for the two tasks probably provide for fewer instances of cost saving on trading personnel, back office personnel, or systems. The fact that the relationship between the central bank and the finance ministry may be different for monetary policy than for exchange rate policy may be seen as a deterrent to bringing the two operations together organizationally. And the proliferation of information systems has made the physical integration of the tasks less of an operational requirement. It is possible for staff in one area to follow developments in one or another market without having to be physically in the same room or operating under the same management.

The evolution of markets and of the policymaking process make it clear that in all central banks, and perhaps in all finance ministries, domestic and foreign considerations will become increasingly integrated. The only question is how. The answer will be affected by some of the considerations I have just noted. In addition, however, it will depend upon the availability of individuals with the experience and outstanding credentials to manage both assignments. In this respect, Alan Holmes was probably a man before his time.

15

FRANCIS H. SCHOTT*

Fixed Versus Fluctuating Exchange Rates

Fixed versus fluctuating exchange rates is a perfect topic for any economist from one very important point of view—it is a hardy perennial. One can write a term paper, master's thesis, doctoral dissertation, or book on the topic without fear of being out of date. You can also sell yourself as a relevant person to any private or government employer dealing with international affairs by having worked on this topic, a decade ago, now, or most likely a decade from now.

The reason is simple yet profound. We know from Adam Smith and David Ricardo that specialization, including that across borders, enhances productivity and potential world welfare. We also know that the optimum currency area is a single world because the implicit factor mobility and absence of currency risk maximize specialization and productivity.

These theoretical observations clash with a world of nation-states, in which currency autonomy is a key attribute of sovereignty. Thus, a single world currency—no exchange rates—is theoretically best, and fixed exchange rates without currency restrictions second-best, in max-

---

*It is an honor as well as a pleasure to contribute to this book in honor of Alan Holmes. I believe I can claim to have been one of Alan's earliest and longest-time friends at the Federal Reserve. He was there as an economist when I joined in 1951 and had advanced to manager of the Federal Reserve Open Market Account when I left in early 1967. Everyone benefited from Holmes's booklet, *The New York Foreign Exchange Market* (1959), which was the first description and analysis since World War II of a fairly freely functioning private foreign exchange market. I was privileged to be Alan's coauthor in the revised and expanded version of that booklet in 1965. In effect he was my mentor. To this day, people tell me how they cut their teeth of international economics knowledge on that booklet.

imizing world output. Fluctuating rates are third-best in that they preserve price signals for resource allocation even while increasing uncertainty. Yet exchange rate fluctuations can and will occur as long as there are nation-states. The fixed/flexible exchange rate topic will go out of fashion only when there is world government, including a single world currency.

History

This brief and highly selective review of the recent history of exchange rates begins with the breakdown of the Bretton Woods fixed-rate system in August 1971, when President Nixon closed the U.S. gold window. This step was followed, in the Smithsonian Agreement of 1973, by a formal devaluation of the U.S. dollar and the acknowledgment of the need for at least a temporary floating of the U.S. dollar. My interpretation of this history is that European countries, following the completion of their post–World War II reconstruction, had increasingly turned toward monetary conservatism whereas the United States had become gun-shy of repeated recessions. Specifically, we wished to secure room for domestic expansion prior to the 1972 presidential election. More basically, with the end of two decades of post–World War II hegemony, the struggle for national economic policy autonomy surfaced fully, and the desired degree of economic sovereignty proved incompatible with fixed exchange rates.

As can be seen in Figure 15.1, a fluctuating exchange rate for the U.S. dollar has now prevailed for two decades. The fluctuations shown in the figure have not been a pure market phenomenon. Rather, they are the result of what is inelegantly known as a "dirty float"—a situation in which central banks and/or governments intervene when deemed appropriate.

During this time, private international trade and capital flows have enormously expanded under the influence of both market-determined exchange rates and major moves toward virtually complete freedom of capital transactions during the early 1980s. Further, in such open economies governments have to acknowledge increasingly that, to the extent exchange rates can still be influenced if not controlled, it is aggregate economic policy through which this influence is exerted, and not exchange intervention per se.

One might point out that the ultimate importance of domestic policy in determining exchange rate trends was well known to the sponsors of

Figure 15.1 Trade-Weighted Exchange Rate of U.S. Dollar

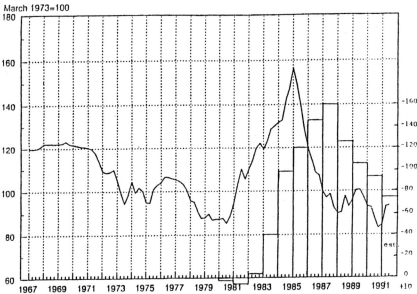

Note: Nominal exchange rate constructed with trade weights of G-10 countries.
Sources: Federal Reserve, Board of Governors, and U.S. Department of Commerce.

the reentry of the United States into official exchange operation in the early 1960s. Many supporters of fixed rates insisted from the beginning that they require domestic monetary conservatism. But it was not to be.

In the mid-1970s, the dollar moved roughly sideways; then, a severe downward slide in the late 1970s probably doomed any possibility of an early return to fixed rates. The decline was induced by strong expansion and excess U.S. inflation compared with that of our major trade partners. By mid-1980, the dollar was down 20 percent over the preceding five years despite the likelihood that the oil price shocks of 1973 and 1979 benefited the dollar on balance.

Under the influence of strong anti-inflationary policy, the dollar then began a spectacular 50 percent, five-year rise until early 1985. This took place despite a massive swing toward deficit in the U.S. current account. Capital inflows because of high U.S. interest rates and because of the attractiveness of an expanding and politically safe U.S. market for foreign investment simply overwhelmed the excess supply of dollars arising from the import surplus. Domestic effects of floating rates were shown clearly, including the help to domestic inflation fighting of a strong dollar and the damage to manufacturing competitiveness of such a dollar. The Reagan administration, ideologically opposed to official intervention, finally relented. The Plaza Agreement of September 1985 signaled a downturn for the U.S. dollar through intervention and policy adjustments in the United States and abroad. By February 1987, in the Louvre Accord, the industrial countries wished to call a halt to the decline in the dollar, but an irregular decline of the dollar continued until recently, with a record low for the floating-rate period in 1990. Only in 1991, with the U.S. recession curbing import demand, was there a significant upward move in the dollar.

One might say that actual U.S. dollar fluctuations have amply vindicated fluctuating exchange rates, at least in this sense: changes as large and persistent as those that occurred would hardly have been accommodated in a fixed-rate system without having had to cause major changes in those domestic policies that the United States in fact preferred.

Theory

The past two decades do not provide a firm theoretical solution to the clash of exchange rate systems. Nevertheless, I believe the record shows that fluctuating rates have worked better than fixed rates would have. Let us review the main theoretical objections to fluctuating rates in the light of experience.

First, there is the objection that fluctuating rates may give incorrect signals about resource allocation. Speculation may push rates in a direction opposite to fundamentals. If, for example, the dollar is driven down contrary to the fundamentals, the cost of inflation and changed resource allocation is incurred unnecessarily and incorrectly.

This problem is compounded by the impossibility of knowing in exactly what direction the fundamentals are pointing. One area of agreement appears to be that the purchasing power parity theorem (PPP) has been proved inoperative in the short run. The theorem states that the exchange rate should move inversely with the respective inflation rates at home and abroad—i.e., with the relative purchasing power of currencies. In the 1980s, the most striking divergence from PPP was no doubt the sharp appreciation of the U.S. dollar early in the decade, which by PPP implied (incorrectly) that our inflation rate fell far short of that of our main trade partners. No doubt the main reason was that capital movements have become increasingly influential to exchange rates and, as already noted, drove the U.S. dollar up in the early 1980s.

Thus, the theoreticians by and large agree that fluctuating rates may give inappropriate short-term signals. But might they also do so in the longer term? That became the number one theoretical problem with the appreciation of the dollar, and it remains an unresolved question even though its urgency has abated with the decline of the dollar. I believe there is a miraculous consensus of economists' answer: The fault was not with the exchange rate system itself but rather with U.S. domestic policy influences on the exchange rate. Specifically, monetary policy and therefore interest rates bore an excessive burden of the restraint as heavy federal deficits were in good part financed by capital inflows. In addition, the combination of federal outlays and deficits was heavily pro-consumption oriented and the national net savings rate was low. Hence, private investment needs also had to be financed by capital inflows. The "incorrectness" of the signals thus conveyed, by the way, also was a widely agreed-upon point—first, because the accumulation of net external debt would eventually have to be reversed through a current account surplus, and second, because the U.S. economy was being put through the painful wringer of a cost purge when the dollar was going to go down eventually anyway to facilitate the required current account adjustment.

The easy answer as to why fluctuating exchange rates are superior—they clear the market—thus became somewhat discredited. Clearing the market is not the only task of exchange rates, perhaps not even the most important task.

The second major theoretical question then became whether a smoothly functioning fluctuating exchange rate system would not actually require international financial cooperation of a high degree. Foreigners hardly wished to argue that the dollar should be fixed again: Had the dollar not been allowed to appreciate, the U.S. current account would not have permitted the huge export gains European and Pacific Rim countries actually made in the 1980s. Rather, foreigners pointed to an inappropriate policy mix in the United States while we urged more expansionary policy abroad. Again, this argument acquires special poignancy because the scale of international trade and capital flows virtually defies coordination through exchange rate policy (i.e., official intervention) alone.

Theory is thus evolving toward the notion that the alleged autonomy for domestic policy obtained via floating rates is somewhat illusory. Avoiding the damaging side effects of a pure price system in the exchanges calls for attention to secondary repercussions of rate volatility.

Policy

Having discussed the relevant theory, let us now turn to policy. Here the main conclusion is that leading governments and central banks have learned to live with fluctuating rates even if they do not like them, which is frequently the case. In other words, there is a sour grapes aspect to the acceptance of fluctuating rates. Without a convincing analytical framework for fixing defensible rates, and desiring domestic room for maneuver, governments largely get out of the way of the markets.

A first important qualification to the general acceptance of fluctuating rates is the continued and frequent exercise of the intervention option by central banks. The Federal Reserve and the Treasury have over the years accumulated tens of billions of foreign exchange reserves, besides the Fed's $30 billion network of reciprocal swap agreements with foreign central banks. You can pick up almost any quarterly report on Treasury–Federal Reserve foreign exchange operations and find acknowledged instances of official operations. These are typically coordinated with foreign official operations aiming at the same objectives. The motivation remains the prevention of excessive swings in exchange rates without resisting basic trends.

Defining such elusive terms as "excessive swings" and "basic trends" remains as challenging as ever, and fluctuating rates enable the authorities to step aside gracefully if intervention does not work. Backing off is far easier than it is in a fixed-rate system, where an abrupt devaluation or revaluation damages prestige along with credibility.

For the same reason—the ability to get out of the way without losing face—governments have been sparing in their use of an intermediate possibility between fixed and floating rates, that is, target zones of (say) 10 percent above and below a defined central rate. Such a system continues to have important defenders. The main advantage of target zones could be that they might generate counterspeculation to an officially undesired trend as the limits are approached. However, getting such market action going depends heavily upon making the targets known, which nowadays no government (including ours) is eager to do, precisely because your intervention might get swamped rather than validated by the market. Thus, rumors of (say) a Japanese-U.S. understanding about an agreed yen–dollar zone remain just that, rumors, and the world remains on fluctuating rates.

And yet, there are truly portentous modifications under way. As was discussed in the introduction to this essay, large single-currency areas such as the United States have great advantages over any exchange rate regime. This is the lesson Western Europe is taking to heart in the drive toward monetary union. The current intense negotiations have been preceded by a gradual convergence of economic policies over the past ten to fifteen years, which have in turn made possible virtual exchange rate stability among European Community (EC) members. Some will argue that German economic might and monetary conservatism have forced inflationary countries (France, Italy) into line, but it is equally plausible that the benefits of price stability are more fully accepted throughout the EC. Thus, convergence carried far enough may lead back to fixed rates!

It is also likely, however, that currency blocs will emerge. Among these, policy coordination rather than convergence may modify floating rates. The three centers are New York, Frankfurt, and Tokyo. Negotiations among the countries represented by these financial capitals turn on trade, fiscal, and monetary policies that minimize the risks of protectionism and world recession. Agreements have tended to run in the direction of policies that are coordinated to move in opposite directions rather than to converge—e.g., expansionist in one, restrictive in the other so as to tame the business cycle in both. There is a similarity to intra-European developments, however, in that domestic economic policy has become fair game in the negotiations while exchange rate policy per se has taken a back seat. Thus, Japanese-U.S. diplomacy deals with "Structural Impediment Initiatives" including financial market regulation and monetary/fiscal policy mix; the exchange rate is simply a fallout item, or influenced only indirectly.

Conclusion

In summary, fluctuating rates have proved to be compatible with strong growth in world trade and investment, even if third-best to a single world currency and an equally unattainable fully credible guarantee of truly fixed rates. In essence, the Bretton Woods system could not survive the drive for national economic policy autonomy once rough equality of major trading countries had been restored following World War II.

But here is the irony. Despite fluctuating rates, the exigencies of a closely integrated trade and financial system are pushing the world toward policy convergence and/or coordination, and away from autonomous domestic policies. In Europe, a single currency may succeed exchange rates of any kind within the next two decades. Among currency blocs, the need to fight the business cycle and protectionism will greatly modify the policy freedom that inspired the turn toward floating rates.

The fixed/flexible exchange rate topic is perpetual. But the terms and conditions of its discussion are showing signs of progress toward a unified and interdependent world economy. If that makes the argument over fixed versus fluctuating rates a less heated one, so much the better.

16

Robert Solomon

International Coordination of National Economic Policies

Economic interdependence among nations has increased greatly. That, you all know. Economic interdependence is measured in various ways. One important measure is that international trade has increased twice as fast as GDP in the world in the last three decades as our economies have become more open to each other. A second measure of increased interdependence is the enormously greater mobility of capital. The increase in international capital flows has far exceeded the increase in trade. A third measure concerns international financial instruments, whose growth has been even more phenomenal. Examples of international derivative instruments are interest rate swaps and currency swaps. These instruments have developed in the last fifteen years, and their existence has facilitated increased flows of funds across national borders.

Some countries are more open than others. As a general rule, the smaller the country, the more open it is. Because of its size, the United States is still one of the less open countries despite the recent internationalization. On the other hand, the small Netherlands has trade flows that exceed half of its GDP. A small open economy is much more exposed to developments abroad.

A large country like the United States, while less directly vulnerable or exposed to what happens abroad, is, however, subject to an extra impact from the rest of the world precisely because it is so large. I call that extra impact a rebound effect. If the United States goes into a recession, this tends to affect output elsewhere much more so, say, than the Netherlands going into a recession. In turn, that effect on economies outside the United States affects American exports. So while the United States is less open and less directly vulnerable, it is subject to a rebound effect that most other countries are not subject to.

What does interdependence mean? The more open a country, the more dependent on policy and economic development in other countries it is. The more open a country, the smaller the impact of domestic policies on its domestic economy because some of the policy impact hits abroad, rather than at home.

The interdependence of policies justifies policy coordination. When countries' policies have a greater impact on each other, there is something to be said for trying to formulate those policies in a way that takes account of those impacts. It is a form of cooperative policymaking, trying to anticipate and take into account the interactions of countries' policies on each other.

Policy coordination involves both the targets of policy and the instruments of policy. The primary objectives of policy are maintaining an adequate rate of growth of real output, GDP; relative price stability; and, often, though not always, a sustainable balance of payments position—a sustainable current account position.

The major instruments of policy are monetary and fiscal policy. In some countries the exchange rate becomes an instrument of policy, but it is not an instrument of policy in the United States.

Some of these targets are complementary. If country A is enjoying an economic expansion, this will tend to spill over to its trade partners and help them achieve a higher rate of economic expansion as well. Similarly for inflation. If a country has a noninflationary economic situation—that is, export prices will not be rising very much—this will tend to help its trade partners hold down the rate of increase of their price levels. Those two targets are complementary in the sense that the success of one country in achieving its targets helps its trade partners achieve theirs.

The balance of payments target, insofar as it is a policy objective, is more a competitive, rather than a complementary, target. By definition, if one country achieves a bigger surplus in its balance of payments, some other country is going to have a larger deficit. The balance of payments is, in principle, a zero sum game, and insofar as the current account of the balance of payments is a policy target, one has to look at it in that way: that not all countries can move toward surplus together—or to a deficit.

What policy coordination comes down to is essentially an attempt to keep these policy targets compatible among countries. This process of policy coordination does not necessarily involve a fine tuning of policies. Fine tuning is not held in favor these days, but how one defines fine tuning is not clear. One person's fine tuning is another person's intelligent policy action. Nevertheless, what is involved here are medium-term policies.

The institution by which policy is coordinated is in meetings held three times a year, primarily among the finance ministers and central bank governors of the seven major industrial countries. The legwork behind those meetings at the top policy level is done by the deputies of these finance ministers, with the very important technical input from the International Monetary Fund, whose economic counselor participates in those meetings of the deputies of the Group of Seven.

Some people and countries, especially countries outside the Group of Seven, might feel that the Group of Seven is too exclusive a club. After all, the others have an interest in what happens in the Group of Seven and would like to have some say in the process. A number of us have recommended that somehow this whole process, while it has to be done in a relatively small group, should be related to what goes on in the International Monetary Fund. The process ought to be embedded somehow in the Fund. Perhaps that can happen in time. The Fund already plays a role in the process, as mentioned earlier, and other countries should be given an opportunity to have some input to this coordination process in which they have a stake.

These finance ministers and central bankers who meet three times a year—and more often if necessary—do not have to make a decision about policies every time they meet. Often they meet and nothing happens. But it is useful for them to meet regularly so as to monitor what is going on in their economies and to monitor the interactions among their economies so that they can act when it is necessary and desirable.

An analogy that has been made is that you can walk by a firehouse and you see these people sitting around just looking up in the air, or playing cards, and they are not doing anything, and you say to yourself, "Why in the world are we paying these firefighters not to do anything—just to sit around and enjoy themselves?" But when a fire breaks out and the alarm rings, they show that they have a function in the world and it is worthwhile keeping them in their firehouse and keeping them at their function.

The regular meetings of the Group of Seven, at which sometimes nothing happens, are analogous to the scene at the firehouse. Those meetings will sometimes produce a set of coordinated policy actions that can benefit the world, as explained below.

The theoretical justification for coordination is the existence of externalities. The policy interactions of interdependent economies create externalities among them, and when externalities exist, then one cannot depend purely on market mechanisms. One needs some form of interference with market mechanisms. An example of a negative externality is what happens in a stadium when people stand up in order to see better. The people in the front row stand up, and then the people behind them have to stand up; pretty soon everybody in the stadium is standing up. They would all be just as well off if nobody had stood up. The rising of the people in the front row imposed a cost on those behind, preventing them from seeing, or requiring them to stand when they would presumably prefer to sit. You need a cooperative agreement among the people in the stadium so that they will understand the externality, to make everyone as well off as possible.

The same is true, given the externalities I have mentioned earlier, in economic policy. The costs and benefits that countries impose on each other because of the openness of their economies need some form of extramarket activity to deal with that externality, and that is what these consultations about economic coordination come to.

Examples of Lack of International Cooperation

A couple of dramatic examples of the failure to engage in this type of international economic coordination are worth noting. The first one occurred in 1972–73. In 1972, all the major industrial countries stimulated their domestic demand. There had been a slowing down in economic activity—the United States actually had a recession in 1969–70 and the other economies slowed down—and all of a sudden major countries adopted expansionary monetary and fiscal policies without taking account of the policies that their trading partners were adopting. As they all began to expand at the same time, the figures show that for the G–7 countries together, GDP was growing at a rate of about 6 percent a year, which is a very rapid rate of growth. The result was an enormous acceleration in the prices of raw materials. Commodity prices rose very, very rapidly in 1972–73 and on into 1974, starting even before the very big increase in oil prices—the first so-called oil shock—which occurred at the end of 1973.

Inflation got going in the world as a result of this combined expansion in the economies of the seven major industrial countries. If international coordination had existed and countries had looked at each other's policies, they might have become aware of this inflationary danger and cut back a bit on their expansionary policies, thereby preventing that rapid inflation from occurring.

The other major example of the lack of international policy coordination came in 1981–82, following the second oil shock. Oil prices rose very rapidly in 1979–80 and inflation again got worse. But this time the major countries found themselves in recession. They were in recession partly because they had adopted fairly stringent restrictive fiscal and monetary policies to try to counteract the inflation. So, here again, countries failed to take account of the policies that their trade partners, the other members of the Group of Seven, were adopting. While each of them had a restrictive policy to hold back domestic demand and try, therefore, to overcome the inflation, what they did not count on was that their exports were going to decrease because their trade partners were also restricting. The result was a much worse recession than they had counted on. International policy coordination, which would have involved a combined examination of their policies and their potential effects, might have at least moderated that worldwide slowdown.

These examples make the potential benefits of successful international policy cooperation obvious. Coordination helps countries to achieve their targets of reasonably rapid growth, price stability, and sustaining their balance of payments. Unfortunately, gains cannot be quantified very well, so the positive effects of international policy coordination remain an area of judgment.

Obstacles to Policy Coordination

If international policy coordination offers significant benefits, why is there so little of it? To understand why, one must understand the major obstacles to policy coordination, some of which are real and some of which are imagined.

Let me first address two imagined obstacles: Some people have said that you cannot expect the process to be successful because it requires countries to give up some of their sovereignty. I think this is a false conception of an obstacle. Countries have a sovereign right to make policy, to make policy in a cooperative way or take account of the actions of other countries before deciding on their own fiscal and monetary policy. What I would say is that countries are using their sovereign right to cooperate—that is, their sovereign right to take account of what policies other countries adopt and intended to adopt. But that loss-of-sovereignty point has been made by a number of critics of this consultation process, so I mention it to you.

One could say that the very process of economic interdependence that I mentioned at the outset by itself weakens countries' sovereignty in the sense that their policy instruments have less impact on their own countries than in the past. There is nothing in this process of policy coordination that requires nations' policymakers to cede their decision-making power. Coordination simply requires that they make those decisions in the light of policy decisions they expect to be made by policymakers of other countries.

A second imagined argument is that the coordination process requires countries to give up their self-interest, to be altruistic, and to adopt policies in the interest of other people. I hope it is clear from what I have said so far that that is also a false accusation about the process.

Let us now consider two real obstacles. One is that the United States is limited in its ability to use fiscal policy. The large budget deficit that the United States has had since early in the 1980s has immobilized its fiscal policy. The United States has just been through the first recession since the 1960s for which the U.S. government has undertaken no significant fiscal policy action to try to accelerate a recovery. On the contrary, the focus of fiscal policy is on how to reduce the budget deficit.

Another real obstacle is how to coordinate alternative visions of how the world works. Putting it more formally, since policymakers in different countries have different models of how their economies operate, it is very difficult to agree on compatible policies. In an extreme example, if the finance minister of country A believes that an increased budget deficit has a contractionary influence, and policymakers in country B believe that an increased budget deficit is an expansionary policy instrument, they are unlikely to agree on policy. Insofar as these different visions exist, there are going to be disagreements about the policy coordination process. In time, such differences should be reduced. As countries meet together, their views as to how policies affect targets are likely to change.

Conclusion

It follows that the world has everything to gain and nothing to lose from international economic policy coordination. The trend toward increasing interdependence, which is likely to go on, enhances the payoff from successful coordination. However, it is useful to remember that there are times when there is nothing for the coordinators to do, just as there are occasions when firefighters remain idle.

Index

About the Contributors

Richard V. Adams is a former vice president and product manager of securities trading at Kidder, Peabody & Co., Inc. He has extensive experience in trading government and other fixed income securities and working with foreign exchange. He has been special assistant to the U.S. secretary of the Treasury for debt management and has held positions in several banks including one of the largest U.S. banks and a major Arab bank. He holds a B.A. from Macalester College and an M.B.A. from Indiana University and has published articles in *Money Manager, Bankers Monthly,* and *American Banker.*

Stephen H. Axilrod is vice chairman of Nikko Securities International in New York and adviser to Nikko's Tokyo-based parent as well as to Nikko Investment Trust and Management Co. He writes a monthly column on policy and market developments for the *Japan Economic Journal* and is a columnist for *American Banker.* He is on the investment committee of the Japan Society and serves on special boards at Brandeis University and Arizona State University. He served the Board of Governors of the Federal Reserve as staff director for monetary and financial policy and was also staff director as well as secretary of the Federal Open Market Committee.

David Colander is the Christian A. Johnson Distinguished Professor of Economics at Middlebury College. Besides his academic experience he has been a consultant for Congress, a Brookings Policy Fellow, and a research scholar at Oxford University. He is the author or editor of twenty books and over seventy articles on a variety of subjects, all related to maintaining a close connection between real-world institutions and economic theory. He has recently done methodological work on the lost art of economics and published a principles textbbook.

Dewey Daane is the inaugural holder of the Alan Holmes Visiting Professorship of Economics at Middlebury College and is the Frank K. Houston Professor of Finance Emeritus at the Owen Graduate School of Management at Vanderbilt University. He is a retired governor of the Federal Reserve System, where he was a member of the Board for eleven years. Prior to that, he had been deputy undersecretary of the Treasury for Monetary Affairs and assistant (for debt management) to the secretary of the Treasury. For sixteen years he was an officer and director of Commerce Union Bank (now NationsBank). He is currently a public director of the National Futures Association and is a former director of the Chicago Board of Trade. His interests include international monetary economics, monetary and fiscal policy, and financial structure. He has a Ph.D. from Harvard.

Margaret (Gretchen) Greene is senior vice president in the foreign exchange area of the Federal Reserve Bank of New York. She is one of only a few people in the United States who have carried official responsibility for exchange rate policy since the beginning of the floating exchange rate period for the dollar in 1971. She regularly represents the Federal Reserve at meetings of the Bank for International Settlements, international meetings of the Forex Association, and other international meetings. She has written numerous articles on international finance for professional publications as well as for the Federal Reserve Bank of New York publications. She is also a frequent speaker and panelist at meetings of international and national associations and a regular lecturer for courses in international finance at the Owen Graduate School of Management at Vanderbilt University as well as at other colleges and universities. She holds a Ph.D. in economics from Columbia University.

Robert C. Holland was, until 1990, president of the Committee for Economic Development, a nonprofit organization in Washington devoted to the study of public policy problems, and is currently its senior economic consultant. Before joining that organization, he was with the Federal Reserve, as a member of the Board of Governors from 1973 till 1976 and before that in various professional and managerial positions on the Board's staff and at the Federal Reserve Bank of Chicago. He has written and spoken extensively on banking, finance, and economic development. He holds a Ph.D. in economics from the University of Pennsylvania and an honorary Doctor of Laws from the University of Nebraska. He has served on the boards of numerous academic and non-academic organizations.

David M. Jones is executive vice president and chief economist of Aubrey G. Lanston & Co., Inc., specialists in government securities. He writes the weekly Lanston financial letter, is a regular commentator on Federal Reserve policy and the bond market on Cable News Network's "Business Morning," and has been a frequent guest on the MacNeil/Lehrer show. He has also appeared on "Wall Street Week," the "Nightly Business Report," CBS's "Morning News" and "Face the Nation" programs, NBC's "Today," and CNN's "Moneyline" show. He is the author of *Fed Watching and Interest-Rate Projections: A Practical Guide,* and *The Politics of Money: The Fed Under Alan Greenspan.* Before going to Lanston he was an economist with the Federal Reserve Bank of New York and vice president of the Irving Trust Co. Dr. Jones has also lectured at institutions such as the University of Wisconsin Graduate School of Banking and the University of Michigan Public Finance Institute.

Eugene A. Leonard is president of the Corporation for Financial Risk Management. He consults on economic and financial activities including money and interest rate risk management. Between 1961 and 1977 he was with the Federal Reserve Bank of St. Louis in a series of capacities including economist, manager of the Memphis branch and first vice president. He also served as assistant secretary to the Board of Governors of the Federal Reserve System in Washington. He holds a Ph.D. in economics from the University of Missouri at Columbia.

Bruce K. MacLaury has been president of the Brookings Institution since 1977. Before that he held a variety of positions at the Federal Reserve Banks of New York and Minneapolis. He has also been deputy undersecretary of the U.S. Treasury for Monetary Affairs and has been a staff member of the Organization for Economic Cooperation and Development. He is a trustee of the Joint Council on Economic Education and the Committee for Economic Development and is a member of the Council on Foreign Relations. He is a consultant to the General Accounting Office and is a director of several organizations including St. Paul Companies Inc., Hudson Corp., the American Express Bank, Ltd., and the Vanguard Funds. He holds a Ph.D. in economics from Harvard University.

Scott E. Pardee is chairman of Yamaichi International (America), Inc., providing a broad range of financial services in securities brokerage and dealing, investment banking, and research. He has been with the Federal Reserve Bank of New York in a series of positions, including manager for foreign operations of the Federal Open Market Committee, and has managed the foreign exchange activities of the Federal Reserve and the U.S. Treasury. He has been executive vice president of the Discount Corporation of New York, a primary dealer in government securities, and has been a director of the American International Group, a diversified insurance company. He holds a Ph.D. in economics from MIT and has taught at MIT, New York University, the American Institute of Banking, and the Columbia Business School.

John Rau is dean of the School of Business of Indiana University. Before accepting that position, he was chairman of the Banking Research Center and a visiting scholar at Northwestern University's J.L. Kellogg Graduate School of Management. His areas of interest are the financial institutions strategy and the public policy dimensions of the global financial system. He was formerly president and chief executive office of the LaSalle National Bank in Chicago, of which he is now a director. He has held many banking positions at the First National Bank of Chicago and the Exchange National Bank. He is senior adviser to the Chicago Clearing House Association and has been a member of the advisory board of the American Enterprise Institute's commission on financial system reform.

Francis H. Schott is a corporate director and a consultant specializing in economic and financial advice and studies. He retired in 1991 from the Equitable Life Assurance Society where he was senior vice president and chief economist as well as a member of the Investment Policy Committee and a director of a wholly owned subsidiary, Equitable Variable Life Insurance. Among his current posts are director and member of the investment committee of Mutual of America, director and member of the dividend and audit committees of the New Germany Fund, and director of the Federal Home Loan Bank of New York. He is a former research and foreign department officer of the

Federal Reserve Bank of New York. He publishes frequently on life insurance cash flow and liquidity, interest rates, and financial markets, and his views are often solicited by the *Wall Street Journal*, the *New York Times*, and *Business Week*. He holds a Ph.D. in economics from Princeton University.

Robert Solomon is a guest scholar at the Brookings Institution and president of RS Associates, Inc., publisher of the monthly *International Economic Letter*, and is also an economic consultant. He is the author of *The International Monetary System, 1945-1981*, published by Harper & Row, and of numerous articles in professional journals. His latest book, *The Transformation of the World Economy, 1980-1993*, was published by Macmillan in early 1994. He also writes columns for the *Journal of Commerce* and testifies before congressional committees. He was with the Federal Reserve Board for nearly thirty years, serving in both its domestic and international activities, and became adviser to the Board and director of its Division of International Finance. On leave from the Board, he was senior staff economist at the Council of Economic Advisers in 1963-64 and served as a vice chairman of the deputies of the Committee on Reform of the International Monetary System in 1972-74. He holds a Ph.D. from Harvard University.

Peter D. Sternlight was executive vice president in charge of Open Market Operations at the Federal Reserve Bank of New York until he retired in December 1992. He was also manager of domestic operations of the Open Market Account and reported to the Federal Open Market Committee. He worked for the Federal Reserve in various capacities since 1950. He has also been a consultant and deputy undersecretary for Monetary Affairs at the U.S. Treasury. He holds a Ph.D. in economics from Harvard University.

Paul A. Volcker is chairman of James D. Wolfensohn, Inc., and Frederick H. Schultz Professor of International Economic Policy at Princeton University. He was chairman of the Board of Governors of the Federal Reserve from 1979 to 1987, and has served in federal government under five presidents, having been president of the Federal Reserve Bank of New York and undersecretary for Monetary Affairs at the U.S. Treasury. He is chairman of several organizations, such as the Trilateral Commission and the Group of Thirty, and is a trustee or member of the boards of the Council on Foreign Relations, the Aspen Institute, the Japan Society, the American Council on Germany, the American Assembly, and the Rand Corporation. He is also on the board of directors of Nestlé, ICI, MBIA, the Prudential Insurance Company, and the American Stock Exchange. Mr. Volcker holds honorary degrees from a number of universities, including Harvard and Princeton.

Dennis Weatherstone is chairman of the board and chief executive officer of J.P. Morgan & Co. He joined Guaranty Trust Company, a predecessor of J.P. Morgan, in 1946 in London, where he served in various capacities until being assigned to Morgan's New York headquarters in 1971. He is a director of General Motors, Merck & Co., the Institute for International Economics, the International Monetary Conference, and the Association of Reserve City Bankers, and serves many financial and banking organizations, such as The Business Council. In 1990 he was knighted, receiving the designation of Knight Commander of the Order of the British Empire. He is an associate of the Institute of Chartered Secretaries and Administrators and a fellow of the Institute of Bankers.

Albert M. Wojnilower is senior adviser of First Boston Investment Management Group, having been chief economist of First Boston from 1964 to 1986. Before joining First Boston he was an economist for First National City Bank and for the Federal Reserve Bank of New York. He is well known in the financial community for interest rate forecasts that departed from the consensus but turned out to be correct. His essays and articles on finance have been published by, among others, the *Encyclopedia Britannica*, the National Bureau of Economic Research, the Federal Reserve Bank of New York, and the Brookings Institution. He has been an adjunct professor of finance at New York University and a director of the American Finance Association. He holds a Ph.D. from Columbia University.